Editor-in-Chief and Founder:
Lyndon H. LaRouche, Jr.
Editorial Board: *Lyndon H. LaRouche, Jr. , Helga Zepp-LaRouche, Robert Ingraham, Tony Papert, Gerald Rose, Dennis Small, Jeffrey Steinberg, William Wertz*
Co-Editors: *Robert Ingraham, Tony Papert*
Technology: *Marsha Freeman*
Transcriptions: *Katherine Notley*
Ebooks: *Richard Burden*
Graphics: *Alan Yue*
Photos: *Stuart Lewis*
Circulation Manager: *Stanley Ezrol*

INTELLIGENCE DIRECTORS
Economics: *Marcia Merry Baker, Paul Gallagher*
History: *Anton Chaitkin*
Ibero-America: *Dennis Small*
Russia and Eastern Europe: *Rachel Douglas*
United States: *Debra Freeman*

INTERNATIONAL BUREAUS
Bogotá: *Miriam Redondo*
Berlin: *Rainer Apel*
Copenhagen: *Tom Gillesberg*
Lima: *Sara Madueño*
Melbourne: *Robert Barwick*
Mexico City: *Gerardo Castilleja Chávez*
New Delhi: *Ramtanu Maitra*
Paris: *Christine Bierre*
Stockholm: *Ulf Sandmark*
United Nations, N.Y.C.: *Leni Rubinstein*
Washington, D.C.: *William Jones*
Wiesbaden: *Göran Haglund*

ON THE WEB
e-mail: eirns@larouchepub.com
www.larouchepub.com
www.executiveintelligencereview.com
www.larouchepub.com/eiw
Webmaster: *John Sigerson*
Assistant Webmaster: *George Hollis*
Editor, Arabic-language edition: *Hussein Askary*

EIR (ISSN 0273-6314) *is published weekly (50 issues), by EIR News Service, Inc., P.O. Box 17390, Washington, D.C. 20041-0390. (703) 297-8434*

European Headquarters: E.I.R. GmbH, Postfach Bahnstrasse 9a, D-65205, Wiesbaden, Germany
Tel: 49-611-73650
Homepage: http://www.eir.de
e-mail: info@eir.de
Director: Georg Neudecker

Montreal, Canada: 514-461-1557
eir@eircanada.ca

Denmark: EIR - Danmark, Sankt Knuds Vej 11, basement left, DK-1903 Frederiksberg, Denmark. Tel.: +45 35 43 60 40, Fax: +45 35 43 87 57. e-mail: eirdk@hotmail.com.

Mexico City: EIR, Sor Juana Inés de la Cruz 242-2 Col. Agricultura C.P. 11360 Delegación M. Hidalgo, México D.F. Tel. (5525) 5318-2301 eirmexico@gmail.com

The Next Steps for Mankind

Trump and Putin: The New Paradigm in Action

July 16—The historic summit today between Presidents Donald Trump and Vladimir Putin marks a dramatic phase-shift in history. It is the result of a long, difficult battle, led in no small part by Lyndon LaRouche over the past fifty years, to create an alignment of interests among the great nations and cultures of history as the necessary and sufficient force required to end the tyranny of the British empire once and for all. In particular, LaRouche posed that cooperation among "Four Powers"—Russia, China, India, and the United States (which represents the distillation of the best of European culture)—could replace the broken Western financial system centered in London and Wall Street, with a new paradigm, based not on monetary power and colonial wars, but on a credit system to bring peace and prosperity through mutual development for all nations.

Before stepping into the private, one-on-one meeting with Putin, Trump told the press that they would be discussing many things, mentioning, in particular, that Russia and the United States were cooperating with "our mutual friend President Xi."

The two Presidents met the press after a two-and-a-half-hour private discussion and a luncheon with their aides. They both confronted the "foolishness" and "danger" of allowing the relations between the two leading nuclear powers to continue to deteriorate. Putin noted that "the current tension, the tense atmo-

kremlin.ru

Presidents Donald Trump and Vladimir Putin at the Helsinki summit, July 16, 2018.

sphere, essentially has no solid reason behind it. The Cold War is a thing of past. The era of acute ideological confrontation of the two countries is a thing of remote past, is a vestige of the past." He proposed re-establishing the anti-terrorism working group, and setting up three joint working groups of experts to work on solutions to the fundamental issues: (1) cyber-security, to get to the truth of the cyber warfare being used by the "Get Trump" task force under Robert Mueller to remove Trump from office and provoke war with Russia; (2) a working group of business leaders to expand cooperation, noting that over 500 leading U.S. business leaders attended the St. Petersburg International Economic Forum in May; and (3) a working group of political and military experts, to look for ways to collaborate on the serious issues facing mankind around the world.

Trump, in his statement, said he was determined to "continue the proud tradition of bold American diplomacy. From the earliest days of our republic, American leaders have understood that diplomacy and engagement is preferable to conflict and hostility." He said that the relationship between the two nations "has never been worse than it is now. However, that changed, as of about four hours ago," adding that "I would rather take a political risk in pursuit of peace than to risk peace in pursuit of politics."

The U.S. and British media were their normal, hysterical frauds, but both Trump and Putin countered their lies forcefully. Asked if Russia had any "compromising material on President Trump or his family," Putin laughed, explaining that he hadn't even known that Trump had been in the country at the time written about in the Steele dossier lies, concluding that "it's difficult to imagine utter nonsense of a bigger scale than this."

When Associated Press demanded that Trump denounce Putin for interfering in the U.S. election, Trump shot back, asking why the FBI never took the supposedly hacked DNC server. "Why was the FBI told to leave the office of the Democratic National Committee? I've been wondering that. I've been asking that for months and months and I've been tweeting it out and calling it out on social media. Where is the server?"

On Syria, Putin said that "the task of establishing peace and reconciliation in this country could be the first showcase example of this successful joint work."

The British assets in the United States are scared. They know they have been caught running a coup against the elected President of the United States on behalf of a foreign power, America's historic enemy, the British empire. Obama's killer CIA chief John Brennan perhaps best demonstrated the hysteria among these traitors, tweeting: "Donald Trump's press conference performance in Helsinki rises to and exceeds the threshold of high crimes and misdemeanors. It was nothing short of treasonous. Not only were Trump's comments imbecilic, he is wholly in the pocket of Putin."

The traitor doth protest too much.

The LaRouche movement is now situated to bring the great powers together, in the spirit of the New Silk Road, to carry forward this historic victory, to build on this optimism as a means to implement the full LaRouche program, using his Four Laws, on an international scale, as the laws that truly cohere with the anti-entropic laws of the universe.

Trump-Putin Summit: What Lyndon LaRouche Proposes for Discussion

by William F. Wertz

This is an edited transcript of opening remarks, delivered by William Wertz, a member of the EIR *editorial board, on the LaRouche PAC Fireside Chat of July 12, 2018. The full* video *is available.*

We're just days away from the summit between President Trump and Russian President Putin. President Trump was just in Brussels; he's now in the UK. He was interviewed by *The Sun*, a British tabloid newspaper, and entered into the fray against the Theresa May government, saying that the policy towards Brexit that May is carrying out is wrong, and that it may kill off any chance of a trade deal between the United States and the UK. So, this is undoubtedly going to explode the whole situation in the United Kingdom, where three Ministers have already quit the government, and a conservative faction of the Tory Party itself has essentially been orchestrating resignations, one after another. Perhaps there will be even more after Trump's visit. After England and Scotland, he will travel to Helsinki on Sunday, for his meeting with Putin on Monday.

LaRouche on International Relations

We don't know precisely what is going to be discussed there, but on the other hand, we know what *should* be discussed there. That is precisely what I want to address this evening by making reference to a document Lyndon LaRouche wrote on March 30, 1984, "Draft Memorandum of Agreement Between the U.S. and the U.S.S.R." That's one year after President Reagan's TV announcement of the Strategic Defense Initiative, a policy Lyndon LaRouche had been instrumental in crafting, both in the United States and through back-channel negotiations with the then Soviet Union, as authorized by the U.S. government itself, by the National Security Council.

In his Memorandum, LaRouche laid out what the policy agreement should be between the United States and the Soviet Union. The Soviet Union later collapsed, in large part because its leadership declined to accept Reagan's proposal for the SDI. In the back-channel negotiations that Lyndon LaRouche was engaged in with the Soviets, when they told him that they would not go with President Reagan's SDI proposal, LaRouche warned the Soviet leadership that the Soviet Union would collapse within five years. And of course, that's precisely what did occur, approximately five years after their rejection of the SDI proposal.

The principles put forward in LaRouche's Memorandum apply today. Of course, there have been many changes since then. There were further proposals made by LaRouche, including the necessity of putting together an alliance among the United States, Russia, China, and India—what LaRouche calls the Four Powers concept, in order to reshape the global economic order and finally defeat the imperial principle embodied in the continuing British Empire. As you can see from the unraveling of the British government right now, we have a unique situation in which President Trump could actually bring about that Four Power alliance, and we could finally defeat our enemy, the British Empire.

Remember, the British Empire has been deeply involved in the ongoing coup attempt against President Trump. It was initiated on the British side by the Government Communications Headquarters (GCHQ), which is their equivalent of the National Security

EDITORIAL

"/>

Agency. GCHQ's actions started in 2015, pretty much just after Trump announced that he was considering running for the Republican nomination for President. So then of course, there was the Steele dossier, written by MI-6 operative Christopher Steele. The entire operation was a major effort on the part of the British to prevent Trump from becoming President in the first place—and then, after being duly elected President, to prevent him from working with Russia and China, in particular, to shape a New Paradigm of economic development on the planet and reverse the policy of deindustrialization and free trade which has wreaked havoc with the United States for more than 45 years, going back to 1971, when President Richard Nixon broke with the Bretton Woods system which had been created at the end of World War II by Franklin Roosevelt.

Peace Through Development

Let me just go through the principles which Lyndon LaRouche put forward in his 1984 Memorandum. As I said, we don't know precisely what will be discussed at the Trump-Putin summit. We know that the two Presidents will have a one-on-one discussion with only translators present at the beginning, as in the Trump-Kim meeting in Singapore; that's the way it was organized. There won't be a bunch of bureaucrats there; Trump and Putin will be able to establish a direct relationship. We know that certain issues such as Syria will most likely be discussed; and there's a concern on the part of both of them for strategic stability in the world in terms of arms policy.

Fundamentally, however, what needs to be discussed are the principles laid out in this memorandum by Lyndon LaRouche back in 1984. I'll just give you some quotes from it. It's a short document, consisting of seven articles. The first four are really sort of a preamble, as in the U.S. Constitution, presenting the principles involved. The **First Article** is **General Conditions for Peace**:

The political foundation for durable peace must be: (a) The unconditional sovereignty of each and all nation-states, and (b) Cooperation among sovereign nation-states to the effect of promoting unlimited opportunities to participate in the benefits of technological progress, to the mutual benefit of each and all.

The most crucial feature of present implementation of such a policy of durable peace is a profound change in the monetary, economic, and political relations between the dominant powers and those relatively subordinated nations often classed as "developing nations." Unless the inequities lingering in the aftermath of modern colonialism are progressively remedied, there can be no durable peace on this planet.

Insofar as the United States and Soviet Union acknowledge the progress of the productive powers of labor throughout the planet to be in the vital strategic interests of each and both, the two powers are bound to that degree and in that way by a common interest.

So, that's the first principle.

Article 2 is **Concrete Technological Policy**, and what LaRouche emphasizes is:

…Technology … is understood to be the indispensable means not only for increasing the potential relative population-density of societies, but as also indispensable to maintaining even any present level of population potential.…

In all aspects of production excepting agriculture, and in respect to industrial goods required by agricultural production, advances in technology are transmitted into the productive process as a whole through the incorporation of improved technologies in capital goods, most emphatically capital goods of the machine-tool or analogous classifications. Therefore, the only means by which a national economy can sustain significant rates of technological progress, is by placing emphasis upon the capital-goods sector of production, and maintaining sufficiently high rates of turnover in that sector to foster high rates of technological innovation in the goods produced.

Under **Article 3: Economic Policies**, he writes:

By supplying increased amounts of high-technology capital goods to developing nations, the exporting economies foster increased rates of turnover in their own most advanced capital-goods sectors of production. As a by-product of such increased rates of turnover in that sub-sector of the exporting nation's production, the rate of improvement of technology in such categories of goods is increased, with great benefits to the internal economy of the exporting nation. Thus, even were the exporting nation to take no profit on such exports, the promotion of higher rates of capital turnover in the capital-goods sector of that exporting nation would increase the productive powers of labor in the exporting nation's economy as a whole, thus supplying great benefit to the exporting nation's economy in that way.

The importer of such advanced capital goods increases the productive powers of labor in the economy of the importing nation. This enables the importing nation to produce its goods at a lower average social cost, and enables it to provide better-quality and cheaper goods as goods of payment to the nations exporting capital goods.

Not only are the causes of simple humanity and general peace served by such policies of practice; the arrangement is equally beneficial to exporting and importing nations.

Finally, **Article 4: International Monetary Policy**:

The only equitable and workable policy for financing of world trade among sovereign states with different economic and social systems is a system of credit based on fixed parities of national currencies, parities fixed by aid of a gold-reserve monetary order among states.

To prevent a gold-reserve system of fixed parities from becoming subject to disabling inflationary spirals, it is necessary to limit the extension of credit within the monetary system to "hard-commodity" categories of lending for import and export of physical goods.

Now, there are a number of articles in which LaRouche puts forward the importance of the Strategic Defense Initiative, which operates on the basis of new physical principles, and the necessity of the scientific discoveries achieved in that effort—the necessity that those scientific discoveries be applied to the civilian economy. In Article 6, he writes, "It must be policy that new such technologies developed in the military area be rapidly introduced into the civilian area." At the end of Article 6, he stresses the following:

The powers jointly agree upon the adoption of two tasks as the common interest of mankind, as well as the specific interest of each of the two powers: (1) The establishment of full economic equity respecting the conditions of individual life in all nations of this planet during a period of not more than 50 years; (2) Man's exploration and colonization of nearby space as the continuing common objective and interest of mankind during and beyond the completion of the first task.

This gives you an outline of what Lyndon LaRouche was advocating as the basis for U.S.-Russian relations back in 1984. The principles involved are precisely the principles that must come into force today with respect to U.S.-Russia relations, with respect to U.S.-China relations, U.S.-India relations, and U.S. relations with any other sovereign nation-state. Those principles define a community of interest among sovereign nation-states as the fundamental principle of the relationship.

The focus, as I think should be clear from what I just read, is capital goods exports from the developed nations to the developing sector of the world, to the mutual benefit of both. The reason is that by exporting capital goods, we re-industrialize the United States. If the United States is going to be exporting capital goods, it has got to gear up its entire economy. By doing that, U.S. jobs are not out-sourced to take advantage of cheap labor abroad. The United States is, in this capital goods focused mode, increasing the productive powers in its own country, and the productive powers of the population in developing sector countries.

You're also laying the basis, through an improvement in their economy, for them to make payment on the capital goods which have been exported to them. Although, as LaRouche points out, even if we didn't get a profit on such capital goods exports, we would benefit by the fact that we were gearing up our economy and we'd have a turnover of capital goods production in our economy which would increase the productive powers of our own labor force.

This principle is something that was essential to the Marshall Plan and to the Bretton Woods system following World War II. During the Marshall Plan, we had such a policy towards Europe and Japan. We improved our economy, but at the same time, it developed the economies of Germany and Japan, and other nations, such that they were then able to pay for the exports which we provided. It really was what the Chinese call a win-win situation. This is the relationship that Roosevelt had in mind in terms of the United States, Russia, China, and India after World War II.

Instead, after Roosevelt's death, the Marshall Plan was primarily oriented towards Western Europe and Japan for Cold War purposes, as set up by Winston Churchill. And, contrary to Roosevelt's intention, we didn't really apply this approach to the rest of the world. Franklin Roosevelt's son, Elliott Roosevelt, wrote a book in 1946 called *As He Saw It*, in which Elliott describes an Aug. 9-12 series of meetings aboard ship off Newfoundland between FDR and Churchill before the United States entered World War II. Roosevelt told Churchill, the U.S. would not be fighting fascist slavery in order to preserve the British Empire. Our intention after the war is to eliminate colonialism, using American methods of economics. FDR was here referring to projects such as the Tennessee Valley Authority and similar undertakings in the United States that were built in 1930s under his Presidency—major infrastructure programs. FDR's vision was not fully carried out after World War II. The colonial powers still insisted upon their entitlement to loot the rest of the world, and Truman was not opposed to that. Roosevelt would have been.

A Community of Principle, a Principle of Community

What we're talking about now is really the potential to re-establish a relationship, not with the Soviet Union, but with Russia as a sovereign nation, and with China as a sovereign nation. India and other nations will join that effort.

One of the problems in Europe today is the European Union. Germany is a nation that formerly excelled in science and technology, and yet Germany today is committed to a Green ideology. Germany has committed itself to the abandonment of coal as a fuel, is abandoning nuclear power for electricity production, and is basically digging itself into a hole. This is something that will take a major effort to reverse. Perhaps, if we put together the Four Power alliance, as envisioned by LaRouche, we can bring Germany and the rest of Europe into a different way of looking at things than they currently do.

A Return to the Bretton Woods System

The last point I will make is this: Article 4 in LaRouche's Memorandum has to do with international monetary policy. Lyndon LaRouche has called for a New Bretton Woods system, which Helga LaRouche highlighted earlier this week in her weekly webcast. We had what was known as the Bretton Woods system after World War II. It was established at an international conference in Bretton Woods, New Hampshire in 1944. Unfortunately, in 1971, it was abandoned by Richard Nixon.

We experienced tremendous rates of industrial progress under the Bretton Woods system. It was a fixed exchange rate system in which the dollar was pegged to a fixed price for gold, which was $35 an ounce. Other currencies were pegged to the dollar, and they could fluctuate within a range of about 1 percent. That stability, in terms of the currencies, allowed for long-term trade agreements. Long-term trade agreements require long-term currency stability; otherwise you can't have 25- or 50-year agreements, because currency speculators will siphon off the benefits of trade by profiting from fluctuations in the value of currencies, and because the actual cost of what was agreed to at the beginning of a trade agreement may have changed down the line.

The Bretton Woods system guarantees the long-term stability. It was a very successful system for that reason, and LaRouche has called for returning to it, although he has indicated that, under new agreements, instead of necessarily using the dollar as the international reserve currency, we may have to define a market basket of hard commodities as the standard—to which the currencies are then pegged.

LaRouche discusses the subject of a market basket of hard commodities in a paper, written on July 18, 2000, "On a Basket of Hard Commodities: Trade Without Currencies," published in *EIR* on August 4 of that year.

EIR Contents

www.larouchepub.com   Volume 45, Number 29, July 20, 2018

Cover This Week

Presidents Trump and Putin meet in Helsinki, July 16, 2018. First Lady Melania Trump looks on.

kremlin.ru

ZEPP-LAROUCHE AT INSTITUT MANDELA

Partnership, Inclusive Growth, and Infrastructure in Africa

Schiller Institute President Helga Zepp-LaRouche spoke at the Institut Mandela in Paris, July 6, 2018, as part of its African Economic and Consular Days—just days before Nelson Mandela's 100th birthday on July 18—at the invitation of its President, Dr. Paul Kananura. An edited transcript follows.

Helga Zepp-LaRouche: *Merci bien.* Ladies and Gentlemen:

There is a profound reason for optimism for the African continent, because with the rise of China, and especially the New Paradigm that emerged with the Belt and Road Initiative, the world has been changing, especially in the last five years at an incredible speed. What China has done with the New Silk Road is to develop a new model of relations among nations, and it is an initiative which is open to all nations of the world.

New bridges and tunnels [**Figure 1**] are now beginning to unite all the continents, and so the new world map is becoming a map of uniting all continents through tunnels and bridges. African development is an integral part of this world development.

With China's offer to have a win-win cooperation, Chinese Foreign Minister Wang Yi reports that 140 nations are now participating, in various degrees, in the spirit of the New Silk Road, which has captured the imagination of many countries in Africa, in Asia, and in Latin America, who see for the first time the concrete possibility of overcoming poverty and underdevelopment, in the short term.

In the last ten, but especially the last five years, China has acted to create development potentials, after centuries of colonialism and decades of IMF condition-

Sébastien Périmony

Helga Zepp-LaRouche addresses the Institut Mandela conference in Paris, July 6, 2018.

alities that had been designed to prevent African and Third World development.

Africa Transformed into Global Powerhouse

With this change in the strategic situation, there is a serious perspective for turning Africa into a global powerhouse. A study published last November indicated that Africa is going to be the next factory of the world. The Russian International Affairs Council (RIAC) has just published new figures showing the positive role of China in the development of Africa. In 2000, the total trade between China and African states was $10 billion only. In 2014, China was already Africa's main trading partner, with a trade volume of $200 billion, and in 2017 China made additional loans of more than $100 billion.

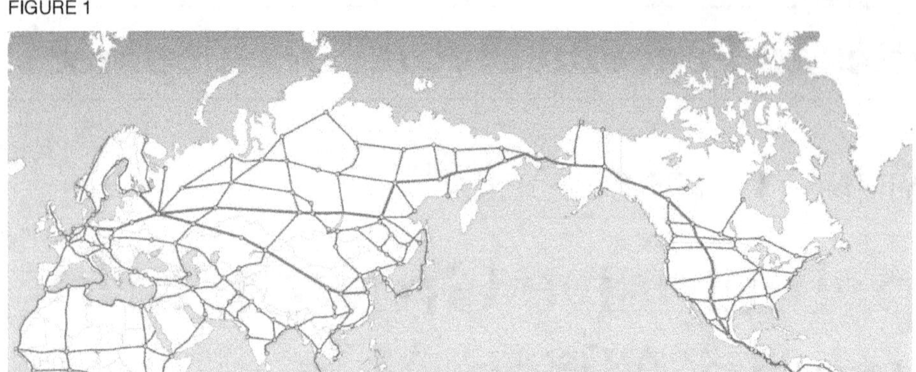

One of the projects recently completed with Chinese help is the Djibouti-Addis Ababa railway. The railway is 750 km long, and now food aid can be brought to areas hit by drought, which was not possible before. And this is just the very beginning. China also has established a China-Africa Development Fund, financed by the China Development Fund. Many other Chinese state banks have been involved in direct investments. Over the last decade, China took part in the creation of more than 100 industrial zones, 40% of which are already operational. By the end of 2016, they had helped to build 5,756 km of railway, 4,335 km of motorways, 9 ports, 14 airports, 34 power stations, and 10 large and 1,000 small hydroelectric power stations.

This coming September, there will be a big China-African Union summit which is expected to take this relationship to a new level.

There is a fundamental change taking place in Africa. The Western countries had refused to invest in a real way in Africa, but with the second largest economy of the world now involved, there is now the prospect for African nations to replicate the Chinese model of development, each in their own African way. However, in terms of infrastructure and industrial development, African nations can take China as a model, which after all, in the last 40 years has undergone an incredible transformation, from being a very, very underdeveloped country, to now being an absolutely breathtaking, dynamic economy.

Africa Challenges Europe and the EU

This is the positive side. On the other side, we are confronted with unprecedented challenges: terrorism, financial turbulence, migrations. A large percentage of the 68.5 million refugees worldwide are migrating from Africa, trying to get through the Sahara, many dying of thirst, or drowning in the Mediterranean, where in the last years, thousands if not tens of thousands have drowned.

Since the refugee crisis escalated in Southwest Asia and Africa in 2015, it has become very clear how deeply disunited the European Union is. Especially in the recent weeks a total government crisis in Germany nearly ended the political career of Chancellor Angela Merkel. There was demonstrated a complete erosion of the EU: No unity, no solidarity, tensions between France and Italy, total tensions between Eastern Europe and Western Europe.

And it is very clear that the EU cannot come up with any solution, because all they could propose at their recent summit was a complete brutalization of the migrant issue: They want to militarize Frontex, the European Border and Coast Guard Agency, to supposedly keep the refugees out of the EU. There were even proposals to use the German army or even NATO forces, to put the refugees into "disembarkment camps," as they call them, either within Europe or in North African states, all of which have already refused to be the hosts of such camps. Pope Francis has compared these camps to the concentration camps of the Nazi period.

What has happened to Western values? What about human rights? What about democracy? The proposals coming out of the EU are *barbarian* proposals; they're not only inhuman, but they also will not work. They will not work. While EU officials are constantly talking about the need to look at the root causes of the refugee crisis, they never do.

The Singapore Summit Model

So, I have a proposal how this can be changed: I call it the "Singapore Summit model." We all have witnessed the very historic summit between President Donald Trump and North Korean leader Kim Jong-un recently in Singapore. It is very clear that it *is* the New Silk Road Spirit which has changed the environment in Asia, which made this summit possible in the way it

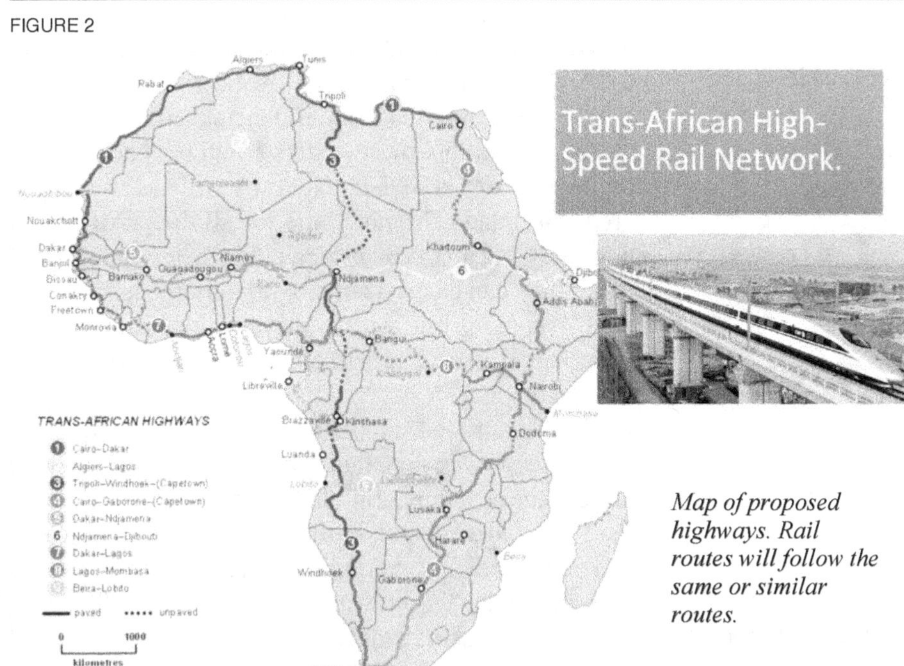

Map of proposed highways. Rail routes will follow the same or similar routes.

took place, and it is also an example of how you can change, within a few months, a hostile adversarial relationship, rife with the potential trigger of a large nuclear war, which was the situation between the United States and North Korea, and turn it into cooperation.

This agreement now includes the denuclearization of North Korea, in exchange for the promise from the United States, China and Russia to help to develop North Korea economically, and turn it into a prosperous nation.

My proposal was that the EU should have changed the agenda of their just concluded summit, and invited Chinese President Xi Jinping, and the African heads of state who have already successfully cooperated with China, and together should have presented a comprehensive crash program for the development of the infrastructure in Africa. [**Figure 2**] The presence of Xi Jinping would have given such a program credibility because China has a record of delivering on development. The idea behind the proposal is to present such an integrated, continental transport plan, a trans-African transport network, which already has been proposed by Foreign Minister Wang Yi in 2014, and reiterated in 2016.

If these leaders—European, African, and Chinese leaders—would announce that it is their intent to institute a crash program for such a development, it would be a signal to the young people who are now running away,

risking their lives in drowning in the Mediterranean, or ending up in concentration camps, to participate in the economic buildup of their own countries.

At the recent visit of French President Macron to Ghana, Ghana's President Nana Addo Dankwa Akufo-Addo basically told Macron that, Ghana doesn't need France's development aid crumbs; what Ghana needs is real investment. He called on youth—rather than trying to get to Europe—to use their youthful energy to build up their own country. This would require training centers, very much like what Franklin D. Roosevelt set up: training, educating, and putting to useful work especially young people in the Civilian Conservation Corps program as part of his New Deal. Such a summit today, with such a declaration of intent, could be like the Singapore Summit, a complete turnaround.

I think we have to also use Xi Jinping's notion of "sustainability." Not meaning "appropriate technologies," however, which in reality means no technology, and not meaning "green" solar and wind power, but instead total infrastructure and industrialization as the new definition of sustainability.

African nations do not have to repeat all the levels and phases of the industrialization of the Western countries, but like China they can leapfrog to the most advanced technologies, such as focussing on high-speed trains, on magnetic levitation, on fourth-generation nuclear power. This plan should include, first, a regional infrastructure investment bank, an African Infrastructure Investment Bank, like the AIIB for Asia. That bank should be paired with national credit mechanisms, or national banks, to manage the internal financing of infrastructure.

Second, there should be an integrated network of high-speed trains, waterways between rivers and lakes, the full development of hydropower projects, fourth-generation nuclear electricity generation, and desalination of large amounts of ocean water for irrigation. Also, as the Ambassador from Ghana already said this morning, there needs be not only the export of raw ma-

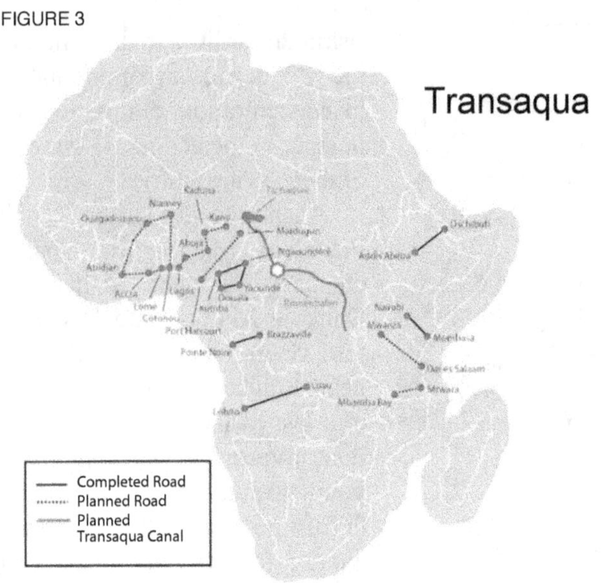

terials, but the production of high-end petrochemicals and metallurgy, and semi-finished and finished products for internal use and for export, that upgrade the value chain in the country.

In addition, there should be a Green Revolution, not in the sense of the Greenies of Europe, but in the sense of the Green Revolution of Jawaharlal Nehru, who transformed the agriculture of India with disease- and drought-resistant plants, and modern food-processing.

Large-scale projects are also needed, such as the proposed tunnel through the Strait of Gibraltar, an eminently doable project. A feasibility study has already been concluded, and a state treaty between Spain and Morocco already exists, so construction could begin almost immediately. A bridge or a tunnel connecting Sicily and Tunisia, which has also been proposed, could be built, with a couple of islands planted in between. These two projects and others like them will serve to integrate the development of Europe with that of Africa. The high-temperature nuclear reactor project in South Africa should be promoted.

The biggest infrastructure project ever, in the history of Africa, is Transaqua. [**Figure 3**] In February of this year, a big conference took place in Abuja, Nigeria, with the presidents of all of the countries of the Lake Chad Basin, who concluded that the only way to save Lake Chad, which now has dried up to only about 10% of its original size, is to refill with waters from some of the tributaries of the Congo River, flowing from 500 meters above the lake.

By gravitation, these waters could be made to flow all the way to Lake Chad. Not only will such a scheme create an inland shipping lane for all the participating countries, but up to 100 billion cubic meters annually of water flow can be used not only to refill the lake and for area irrigation, but also to drive turbines to produce electricity. Lake Chad will once again reach the size of 25 square km.

Transaqua was adopted at the Abuja conference, and a treaty was concluded between PowerChina—a large Chinese engineering firm famous for having built the Three Gorges Dam, so they are very knowledgeable and experienced in making such big projects—together with the Italian engineering firm Bonifica. Italian government representatives at that conference announced that Italy will pay 1.5 million euro to produce a feasibility study within one year. Transaqua is a perfect model for a tripartite cooperation among African nations, China, and in this case, a European nation, Italy.

Construction of Transaqua will be not a long-term project. PowerChina, the lead engineering contractor for the project, announced at the conference that it is confident that it can finish this project in 12 years. It will be an industrialization right in the heart of Africa that will be completely transformational.

Last August, *People's Daily* carried an article about Transaqua, giving credit for the project to the LaRouche movement and the Schiller Institute, because of our work over the last three decades in many conferences, advertising this to many people, and finally getting PowerChina and Bonifica together on it. It's now a state treaty between China and Italy. That article emphasized our role in those efforts.

FIGURE 4

Transaqua is just one of the results of our decades' long work to help to industrialize Africa. Our book-length 1976 report, *The Industrialization of Africa*, is a total plan for the industrialization of Africa, and it was published as a book in 1978. [**Figure 4**] So as you can see, today's exciting developments are not just coming out of the blue. Our movement, from its very beginning,

based on the ideas of my husband, Lyndon LaRouche, has stood for the industrial transformation of the southern hemisphere, because it's the only way to alleviate poverty, and create a decent living standard for all people.

When the *Lagos Plan of Action for the Economic Development of Africa* was published in 1980, my husband wrote a commentary on it, which brought in a very important conceptual approach to tackling the problem of underdevelopment, by creating a continental infrastructure plan, new cities, and science cities, with a strong focus on the education of the youth. We campaigned for this, for four decades. The total work of that 40 year effort went into *The New Silk Road Becomes the World Land-Bridge*, which we published in 2014, after Xi Jinping announced the New Silk Road. And just about one week ago, we released the pre-prints of *The New Silk Road Becomes the World Land-Bridge, Volume 2*, which has an updated plan for how to do this. [**Figure 5**]

We have conducted conferences in Sudan, for the five countries around the Nile, discussing how they could work together on development. And I also addressed an economic summit in Abuja in 1997. [**Figure 6**] In Europe we conducted many campaigns under the title "The Future of Europe Lies in Africa."

Application of the Singapore Model

I think the application of the "Singapore model" is quite possible. Austria's new Chancellor Sebastian Kurz, who until the end of the year is the president of the European Union Council, has announced that he wants to conduct an EU-Africa summit before the end of the year. Now Austria, while having a hard line on the migrants, on the other side, has in the document of the two coalition parties in the government, a chapter discussing Austria's desire to become a hub for the New Silk Road. And there are also many Central and Eastern European nations, Balkan nations, Southern European nations that want to be hubs. For example, Spain and Portugal not only want to be the terminus of the Eurasian Silk Road towards the West, but they want to be hubs to the Portuguese- and Spanish-speaking countries around the world.

If they all cooperate on the New Silk Road, this would be the way to do this, and since the refugee crisis will not go away until the policy is fundamentally changed toward an industrialization of Africa, I think this crisis can be turned into an opportunity. Right now the Schiller Institute—and I would encourage all of you to help us carry this out— is pushing for a full mobilization of all European and African nations that agree, to put pressure on behalf of this perspective and present the EU at its upcoming summit with a con-

Zepp-LaRouche in Sudan (left) and Nigeria (right).

crete outline of the necessary investments, with the participation of China, but also involving other countries, such as India, Japan, even the United States, to do likewise.

Approach it the way China does. China builds a high-speed train—and I saw it with my own eyes, from Lanzhou to Urumqi, in *half a year*—not by building it one step after the other, but by building it simultaneously from 10 or even 20 different places. So, "Partnership, Inclusive Growth and Infrastructure in Africa." If such a concrete plan existed, building could start at many places at the same time.

We have outlined the projects in our two reports. [**Figure 7**] A satellite image of Africa at night [**Figure 8**] shows almost no light emitting from the continent. If we go in the direction I have just suggested, that is, extending the New Silk Road to Africa through a collaborative effort of all nations, then Africa will light up its night sky in a way comparable to the way the United States and Europe do.

Implementing our development approach will turn Africa into a modern, prosperous continent, where all citizens enjoy a safe, and happy and long life. So if we all act together in that spirit, Africa will be the new China with African characteristics. [applause]

FIGURE 7

FIGURE 8

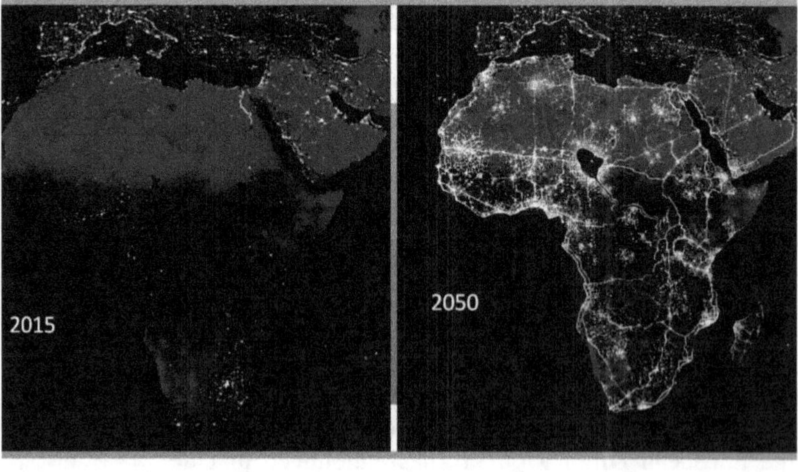

Developing North Korea— Transforming Asia and the World

by Mike Billington

July 15—The diplomatic breakthrough on the Korean Peninsula—driven by the historic summit between South Korean President Moon Jae-in and North Korean Chairman Kim Jong-un on April 27—followed by President Donald Trump's even more historic summit with Kim Jong-un in Singapore on June 12, sets the stage for a development process in North Korea which will facilitate a transformation of the entirety of East Asia, and indeed of the entire world.

Korea Summit Press Pool via AP

North Korea's leader Kim Jong-un (left) and South Korea's President Moon shake hands in the DMZ ahead of their summit at Panmunjom, April 27, 2018.

Moon of South Korea, through his "New Northern Policy," which made the Korea breakthrough possible.

The Trump-Kim summit must be seen in the context of the world-historic transformation taking place internationally through the spirit of the New Silk Road, Xi Jinping's Belt and Road Initiative. Within that framework, President Trump's opening to Russia, China and North Korea has effectively united all of Asia—including Japan, India, and all of Southeast Asia—behind the vision of peace through development. It exemplifies the potential in Lyndon LaRouche's call over a decade ago for a "Four Power" agreement among Russia, China, India and the United

Festering Crisis Turned into Its Opposite

The festering crisis on the Peninsula since the end of the Second World War, and especially after the Korean War of 1950-53—a war which has never been formally resolved—has served the advocates of Empire as a crucial point of division between East and West, with the "war party" within the Anglo-American alliance demanding that all nations line up on one side or the other, maintaining the imperial "divide and conquer" which has served the British Empire historically.

But President Trump has rejected that imperial division of the world, insisting that the United States should be friends with both Russia and China. It is that intention—expressed by Trump's personal friendship with Xi Jinping and his July 16 summit with Vladimir Putin—and a similar view by President

Wikimedia Commons/Dan Scavino, Jr.

President Trump (right) and Kim Jong-un shake hands at their summit in Singapore, June 12, 2018.

An open air roadside market, Chongdan County, North Korea. Private business is an essential aspect of livelihood for most North Koreans.

States, as the necessary combination to overcome and destroy the power of the British Empire and bring about a new paradigm for Mankind.

Other efforts to unite Asia behind a common vision of joint development have been undertaken. But nearly all were stymied by the isolation of North Korea. South Korea considered itself a virtual island, cut off from the Eurasian continent by the division of its country. The development of the vast resources of the Russian Far East, in which China, South Korea and Japan can and must play a crucial role, has also been stymied by the fact that the ostracized North Korea is central to such a collaboration, for both political and geographic reasons. The political divisions across the region that had been aggravated in the post-World War II era by the "with us or against us" dictates of the Cold War, were aggravated further by Presidents Bush and Obama, even after the collapse of the Soviet Union. Now that can and *is* changing.

As I will show, provided the denuclearization process proceeds successfully, and North Korea's security is assured, North Korea is primed to undergo a rapid and powerful economic expansion, which will not only lift the struggling people of North Korea out of their poverty and stagnation, but will benefit peace and development worldwide.

North Korea's Economy

Although some of the popular perceptions about the life of the people in North Korea are accurate—they are indeed very poor, they suffered a severe famine in the 1990s, they live under an oppressive form of government ruled since the 1940s by the Kim family dynasty, and they have been denied many human rights— nonetheless, the most fundamental human right, that of a decent standard of living, has been improving (from a very low level) significantly, especially since the beginning of Kim Jong-un's leadership in 2011. A recent study by William Brown—who served for many years as the leading economic expert on East Asia at the CIA and the National Intelligence Council, now teaching at Georgetown University—is "Special Report: North Korea's Shackled Economy, 2018," published by the National Committee on North Korea in March, 2018. While reporting on the serious deterioration of the industrial plant and equipment and basic infrastructure since the end of support for North Korea from the Soviet Union in 1991, Brown nonetheless points to the "excellent resource base and highly competitive skilled labor" in the country. He also notes:

> The footprint—that is, the existing framework for infrastructure development—is already there, making potential development relatively easy and fast. An ancient civilization with well-developed villages and towns, northern Korea received a large amount of Japanese investment during the colonial occupation (1910-45), including a modern rail system, ports on both its east and west coasts, hydro-electricity, and tele-

A used China Railways DFH3 diesel-hydraulic locomotive purchased for service in North Korea, Oct. 4, 2015.

Yalu River Railroad Bridge half-destroyed by U.S. bombers during the Korea Conflict, Nov. 1950.

Sino-Korean Friendship Bridge across the Yalu River.

phone and telegraph services. This infrastructure avoided damage during World War II but was devastated during the Korean War and then rebuilt in its aftermath. Between 1953 and the mid-1980s, Pyongyang, with substantial assistance from the Soviet Union, Eastern Europe, and later China, added significant thermal electric power, a limited express road system, and petroleum-related energy infrastructure. These have been very poorly maintained, however.

In fact, North Korea, at the time of the Korean War, was by far more developed than the South, which had been primarily the agricultural breadbasket under Japanese occupation, while the North was highly industrialized. The "Korean miracle" under South Korean President Park Chung-Hee (Presidential term 1961-1979) turned a war-torn and impoverished South Korea into the industrial power that it is today. There is no reason that the North cannot be similarly transformed in a relatively short period of time.

Still, the task is formidable. Prof. Brown points to the nearly thirty years of neglect of maintenance of industry and infrastructure since the end of Soviet assistance, and North Korea's focus on its military defenses at the expense of the basic economy. "This neglect," Brown writes, "extends through the rail and road systems, electric power supply, water and sewer systems, heating systems, public health infrastructure and many other areas." Communication systems are better off, he reports, in part due to an Egyptian company, Orascom, which developed a 3G cellular network for the country.

Agriculture is in even greater need of transforma-tion, although Brown notes that agriculture "may hold the key to economic reform given the potential for unleashing productivity gains among North Korea's many farmers." Agricultural productivity in South Korea is between 15 and 20 times higher than in the North. Although much of the country is too mountainous for any agriculture other than grazing, the coastal provinces in the west, and a strip of land along the east coast, contain decent arable land. The collapse of Russian aid, coupled with several natural disasters in the early 1990s, led to a severe famine from 1994 to 1998 in the isolated country, with estimates of deaths by starvation ranging from 500,000 to three million. Malnutrition is still common in the North, although the agricultural base has been largely restored. The emergence of private markets, especially for food, which have been accepted by the Kim Jong-un government, rather than the former policy of total control over food distribution by state distributors, has made food far more accessible to all.

Energy supply is one of the major problems facing the nation. A hydroelectric power plant on the Yalu River on the border with China, built by the Japanese in 1943, and a coal-fired plant in Pukchang, near one of North Korea's plentiful anthracite coal mines, built by the Soviets in 1960, provide over half of the nation's power supply.

Two 1,000 MW light water nuclear power reactors (nuclear weapons proliferation-resistant), which were to be built for North Korea by the United States and South Korea under the 1994 Agreed Framework with the Clinton Administration, would have increased the nation's power supply by as much as 50%. (These reactors were to be built in exchange for freezing construction and operation of nuclear reactors suspected of being part of a covert nuclear weapons program, and for allowing IAEA inspectors into the country, among other things.) When the Bush-Cheney regime came to power, it quickly scrapped the entire Agreed Framework, and construction of the two 1,000 MW reactors was terminated. The Agreed Framework, together with Obama's "strategic patience" policy toward the North, essentially allowed Pyongyang to proceed in building nuclear weapons. North Korea's building of nuclear weapons with a missile delivery system, in turn, was used by the Bush/Obama administrations to justify a build-up of U.S. nuclear forces around China and Russia's Far East, under the false argument that it were needed to defend against North Korea.

North Korea is rich in valuable minerals, which could quickly provide Pyongyang with a source of foreign currency needed to sustain the reconstruction process. Zinc, rare earth metals, limestone, manganese, copper and other metals have been estimated by South Korea's national mining company to have a potential value of $6 trillion. Brown notes, however, that the mines also suffer from neglect, in part due to the lack of electricity needed to prevent flooding.

North Korea has excellent ports, especially on its east coast. The port in the city of Rason in the far northeast, which borders on both Russia and China, has been expanded and modernized over the past decade by both Russian and Chinese interests. While China built a modern road from Jilin Province to the port, providing access to the sea from the land-locked province, Russia reconstructed an old rail connection from Vladivostok to Rason.

In an extremely important experiment in cooperation, Russia, North Korea, and three leading South Korean companies (Hyundai Merchant Marine, steel giant POSCO, and the state rail company KORAIL) formed the Rason Consortium in 2013, which began to ship Russian coal to the port at Rason. The coal was then loaded onto South Korean Hyundai Merchant Marine ships, which took it to South Korea, whereupon it was then transferred onto KORAIL trains for delivery to POSCO steel plants and other locations—a model of the kind of cooperation by which North Korea could be integrated into regional development in a win-win fashion to benefit all parties.

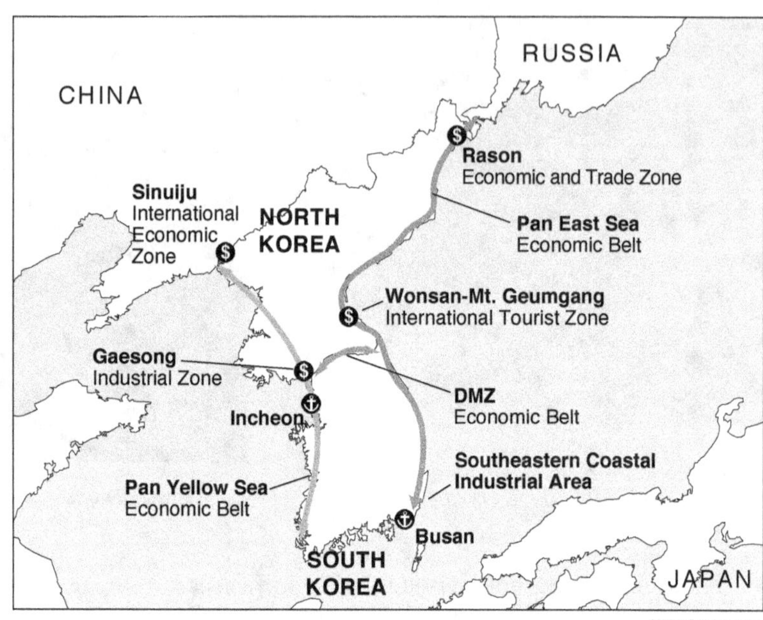

EIRNS/Alan Yue

Korean ports (anchor symbols) and special economic zones (dollar signs).

Progress Toward Cooperation and Peace

Unfortunately, in 2015, President Obama pressured then South Korean President Park Geun-hye to shut down all cooperation with the North, following one of North Korea's (fully predictable) nuclear weapons tests. As a result, the entire Kaesong Industrial Park north of the DMZ, involving 123 South Korean firms with North Korea workers, was summarily closed, while the Rason Consortium also collapsed, although Russia still exports coal to China through the Rason connection.

The impeachment and removal of President Park from office in 2017 was primarily due to a complex corruption scandal. Her decision to shut down all economic relations with the North did inflict serious damage to South Korean businesses and went against the desire for peace between North and South Korea in the South Korean population, contributing to popular support for the impeachment action

President Moon, who was elected in a special election in May 2017 following Park's impeachment, is committed to reopening and expanding the "Sunshine Policy" projects with the North, and much more, although the UN sanctions must be lifted before they can begin. On June 22, 2018, soon after his summit with Kim, and Trump's summit with Kim, Moon visited Moscow. Speaking to the Russian Duma (the lower house of the Federal Assembly), he said:

Regarding Korea-Russia cooperation as the cornerstone of peace on the Korean Peninsula and prosperity in Northeast Asia, I have made wholehearted efforts thus far. Immediately after I was elected President, I spoke by phone to President Putin and sent a special envoy to Russia, the first of such kind by a Korean President, to discuss how to work together

Kim Jong-un (first right) meeting with Sergey Lavrov, Russian Foreign Minister (fourth left), in Pyongyang, North Korea, May 31, 2018.

for the peaceful resolution of the North Korean nuclear issue and the development of the Russian Far East. In addition, I established the Presidential Committee on Northern Economic Cooperation exclusively charged with economic collaboration with Russia to be in step with the Ministry for Development of Russian Far East....

The potential of Russia lies in the deep understanding of human beings. That became the strength of the Russian people who never cave in to any challenge or difficulty.... Like the people of Russia, Koreans are very strong mentally, too. I think this is the reason why our two peoples love Tolstoy.... The dreams of our two countries for the Russian Far East are not different. Striving for peace and prosperity in Eurasia is a mission entrusted to us by the peoples of our two nations.

President Moon then described the historic transformation taking place on the Korean Peninsula, adding:

The active support and cooperation of the Russian Government and people have become a huge force behind this amazing transformation.... I hope that South and North Korea will be able to join in developing the new potential of Eurasia and achieving mutual prosperity of the region.... If the wisdom of North Korea as well as of Russia and South Korea are combined, the dream for a Eurasian era as vast as the Continent will unfold.

On May 31, Russian Foreign Minister Sergey Lavrov visited North Korea, meeting with Chairman Kim, the first Russian official to meet with Kim since he came to power in 2011.

In an interview with China Media Group on June 6, preceding his visit to China for the Shanghai Coopera-

tion Organization summit, President Putin said he looked forward to the Trump-Kim summit, adding: "I do hope that the courageous and mature decision to hold a personal meeting with the North Korean leader Kim Jong-un ... will take place—we will all be waiting for it to produce positive results." He noted that he and Xi Jinping had put forward a joint road map for peace and security in Korea, which included a "double freeze"—that is, for North Korea to freeze all nuclear weapons and missile tests, and for the United States and South Korea to freeze major military exercises, for as long as constructive negotiations and positive actions were taking place.

In fact, this is precisely what has been implemented by Kim Jong-un since the beginning of the year, and by Donald Trump following the June 12 summit with Kim.

Putin also said that "the next stage is multilateral participation of all the interested states," adding that he looked forward to restoring the "trilateral economic projects between Russia and the northern and southern parts of the Korean Peninsula. These will be chiefly infrastructural projects. We are talking about the construction of a railroad (and by the way, China could join these projects as well), between Russia and North and South Korea. We are talking about the installation of a gas pipeline," and other energy projects. In fact, on June 15, Gazprom announced that it had resumed talks with South Korea on building a gas pipeline through the North—a plan that had been initiated in 2011 but suspended when President Park shut down contacts with the North in 2015.

Putin has invited Kim Jong-un to Moscow; this visit is expected to take place before the end of the year.

China's Role

With the collapse of the Soviet Union in 1991, China increasingly became the primary investor in, and trading partner with North Korea, importing huge quantities of coal and minerals, and providing North Korea with oil and machinery. Charts in Brown's report show that in 2006—while South Korea was still trading with the North—China and South Korea together accounted for the vast majority of trade with North Korea. India, Russia, Thailand, Brazil and a few other countries were engaged with North Korea at a lower level. With President Park's shutdown of all business dealings with the North in 2015, the trade figures for 2016 show China with an incredible 91% of the total imports and exports of North Korea. Then, as China joined with the Trump-led sanctions imposed by the UN in 2017, China's trade with the North fell by nearly half.

Nonetheless, Kim Jong-un recognizes that China will be key to a North Korean economic transformation, bringing the New Silk Road process into the country and into the broader region. He has visited Xi Jinping three times since March, twice before the Trump summit and once the week after. It was reported this last week that Kim has invited Xi to attend the North Korean National Day, the 70th anniversary of North Korea's foundation on September 9, 1948. If Xi does attend, it would be the first visit by a Chinese president since Hu Jintao in October 2005, before North Korea began conducting nuclear and missile tests in 2006.

Also visiting Beijing last week, according to the *South China Morning Post*, was Ku Bon-tae, North Korea's vice-minister of external economic affairs, to discuss cooperation in agriculture, rail transport and electricity.

The Rason-Russia railway link, constructed by North and South Koreans along with Russians during the "Sunshine Policy" period between North and South Korea, extended a standard gauge line from Russia to Rajin Port in North Korea.

Moon Jae-in's 'New Economic Map Initiative'

When President Moon and Chairman Kim met at Panmunjom in the DMZ on April 27, Moon handed Kim a computer thumb drive containing his proposed plan for the economic cooperation between South and North Korea. On July 3, the plan was presented to the press, revealing that it goes beyond the joint development of North Korea, to include the integration of North and South Korea with China, Russia, and Central Asia and Europe. The plan presents the idea of creating a virtuous circle of peace and prosperity.

The two primary rail lines to be reconstructed along the now dilapidated routes built during Japanese occupation (1910-1945) will connect South Korea with China along the west coast, and with Russia along the east coast. The west coast line, called the "Yellow Sea Industry/Logistics Belt," will pass through the North Korean capital, Pyongyang, then on to Sinuiju at the Chinese border, across the Yalu River from Dandong in China's Liaoning Province. China recently completed construction of the New Yalu River Bridge connecting Dandong to Sinuiju, to replace the aging Friendship Bridge built by the Japanese to connect Japanese-occupied Korea with the Japanese-occupied region of Manchuria (called Manchuko by the Japanese) in China's Northeast. The North Koreans have yet to build the necessary roads to connect to the new bridge.

The east coast rail line, called the "Pan-East Sea Energy/Resource Belt," will connect South Korea with the ports on the North Korean east coast, then on to Vladivostok, connecting there to the Trans-Siberian Railway. This will complete the concept first presented by Lyndon LaRouche in his 1993 proposal for the New Silk Road, "from Pusan to Rotterdam."

The South Korean proposed plan includes a third "belt"—the "DMZ Peace Belt," which calls for turning the DMZ, the mine-laden, four-kilometer wide region that has been a war-frozen zone for the past 68 years, into a cooperative space for ecological and tourist development.

The unity of all of Asia in building a region of peace through development, with the close participation of the United States, can and must be a model for Southwest Asia and other crisis spots around the world.

Contact the author at mobeir@aol.com.

Stuck in the Old Paradigm, European Governments Face Existential Crisis, with No Solutions

This is the edited transcript of the July 12, 2018 Schiller Institute New Paradigm webcast, an interview with the founder of the Schiller Institutes, Helga Zepp-LaRouche. She was interviewed by Harley Schlanger. A video of the webcast is available.

Harley Schlanger: Hello, I'm Harley Schlanger from the Schiller Institute. Welcome to our webcast this week featuring our founder, Helga Zepp-LaRouche.

This is quite an extraordinary week that's starting to unfold with President Trump's trip to Europe. If you were to read the British press, the *Washington Post*, and *New York Times*—and I don't know that anyone would—but if you do read them, you'll be told that Trump's trip could be the end of NATO, the end of the world as they know it; that Trump is about to sell out to Putin completely. So how better to find out what's actually going on than by speaking with Helga Zepp-LaRouche?

Helga, the NATO conference took place yesterday. There are ongoing meetings. What's your assessment of what's happened so far with President Trump's trip to Europe?

Helga Zepp-LaRouche: He's causing some waves, which is in part good, because NATO lost its purpose for existence when the Soviet Union disintegrated. So I think that if NATO were to dissolve, it would not be a bad thing. There is no real threat from Russia in Europe.

Trump's remarks yesterday about Germany being a hostage of Russia are, I think, more about the interests of American businesses in selling liquefied natural gas from fracking in the United States. The Nord Stream 2 pipeline is, as Trump would normally say, "a good thing," and does not mean European dependency, Ger-

White House/Shealah Craighead

Leaders of six of the twenty-nine NATO member countries at the NATO summit in Brussels, Belgium, July 11, 2018.

many dependency, on Russian energy supplies. I think there he was clearly off in what he said about that. I think that the idea of increasing NATO funding up to 4% of the each nation's GDP, in light of what I just said, does not make any sense either. Hopefully this will all take a different turn very soon. Even though we don't know the full agenda of the July 16 Putin-Trump summit yet, discussion of disarmament is on the table. If the United States and Russia were to come to a reasonable agreement for disarmament and curb the arms race, then NATO would be seen in a different light.

The Upcoming Putin-Trump Summit

The more important meeting is definitely this Putin-Trump meeting. Russia and the United States are the world's two pre-eminent nuclear powers. In a different way, the world's two largest economies—the United States and China—are also strategically relevant discussion issues; all other issues are really less important, despite the hysteria, on the side of the neo-liberal/neo-con faction of the West. It's sometimes really amusing to see how these Western governments, which are stuck in the old paradigm, are completely unable to think constructively about the future. One very good example of that failure is what is happening to Theresa May's British government right now—her government is clearly falling apart.

So, we'll see. Trump will leave for Great Britain today, primarily to play golf, and also to have a meeting with the Queen—I'm making a little bit of fun of it, but the May government may not even exist by the end of his visit. So there is clearly the need to have a completely different approach.

Schlanger: I think it should be obvious to President Trump that the British are not exactly his friends, given the exposé of the British role in launching Russiagate, and then also, the May government has made a series of provocations—the Skripal affair and the accusation of Syrian government use of chemical warfare in Douma, which accusation has now been dismissed by the Organization for the Prohibition of Chemical Weapons (OPCW).

So, he's going into England in a very interesting situation. You mentioned the collapse of the government there. Is there anything emerging on the horizon that would be hopeful in Britain?

Zepp-LaRouche: There may be new elections. If Labour Party leader Jeremy Corbyn were to become prime minister, that would definitely be a turn for the better, and that is obviously what many Tories are freaked out about. The recently resigned Foreign Secretary, Boris Johnson, is engaged in a power game. He wants to be prime minister, but Johnson has many ene-

Leaders of six of the twenty-nine NATO member countries at the NATO summit in Brussels, Belgium, July 11, 2018.

CC/Arno Mikkor

Boris Johnson, former UK Foreign Secretary.

Jeremy Corbyn

Jeremy Corbyn, Leader of the British Labour Party.

mies, so that may not go so easily. Five high-level Tories have left May's cabinet. Some people in London are saying that there might be daily resignations until May is actually out.

One of the big issues in the background is what will happen to the City of London. Theresa May is supposed to present a White Paper this afternoon with her specific proposals for a so-called "soft" Brexit. The "soft" Brexit would mean that the British can pick and choose in which European institutions they want to remain and which they don't, so it's something which for sure will not go so easily with the EU, for the reason that if one country, Great Britain, is allowed to do that, then the appetite of others to do likewise may actually increase. The so-called "hard" Brexit faction is also linked to the City of London, at least in the Tory Party.

So, I think the best thing that could happen in Great Britain would be if the new elections were to lead to an election victory of Corbyn—there would be something closer to a decent policy for the first time in the UK.

A New Bretton Woods Monetary System

The British role in Russiagate and in other efforts against Trump to get him out of the White House—either by a coup or impeachment, or by some other means—has been sustained and intense. However, this is falling apart. The role of the British is definitely weakened. The role of the British has been exposed in Russia, especially. So I think the really important thing is the discussions between Trump and Putin. The world is full of urgent problems: a financial crash could be caused by a hard Brexit, but it could also be triggered by some other banking crisis. Deutsche Bank, for example, is not in good condition; neither is the situation of corporate debt. All of these situations really require a different approach, and therefore our answer to all of this, is to have a New Bretton Woods system, which is urgently required. We have to reestablish stability in the financial system as it existed before 1971. If the Western financial system collapses in an uncontrolled way, it could trigger chaos around the globe.

I know that the Chinese are extremely concerned about fixing the global financial system. We, the Schiller Institute, right now are promoting the idea of going back to the Bretton Woods idea of Franklin D. Roosevelt—a New Bretton Woods in the context of a global reform of the financial system: Glass-Steagall, the separation of the banks in the tradition of Roosevelt; a national bank in each country; new credit mechanisms for long-term lending for investment in industry; and then having clearing houses among the different national banking systems for international long-term investment in the context of the Belt and Road Initiative, the New Silk Road. I think it's very urgent that these things be addressed. The only impetus, as of right now, could come from both a combination of Putin and Trump and Trump and the Chinese, if Trump would take up some of the proposals of China, on how to solve the trade imbalance.

We have to elevate the discussion and not fall into a squabble of one country against the other in a zero-sum game. We need a New Paradigm, the life's work of my husband Lyndon LaRouche, for which he has made detailed proposals and interventions going back many years. I think the first comprehensive proposal he made for reform of the financial system was in 1975, when he proposed an International Development Bank to replace the IMF. The Four Power agreement for a New Bretton Woods, as a starting point, which other countries can then join in with, is the way to go.

It's eminently feasible, because the New Silk Road does exist; it has created a completely different dynamic in the world, and therefore, I would invite all of you, our viewers, to help us to spread this idea, because we need a discussion of how to get out of this crisis.

Schlanger: Helga, given your role in fighting for this New Paradigm and promoting the idea of the Four Power agreement, to what extent do you think there is in China, and in Russia, a discussion process going on about a New Bretton Woods replacing the collapsing financial order of the trans-Atlantic system? Is that implicit or explicit in the discussions that are going on?

Zepp-LaRouche: I'm not entirely sure. I know that President Xi Jinping has addressed the issue of global financial governance on many occasions in the recent month; I know that the Chinese are extremely worried about the present trade tensions between the United States and China going out of control; and I think that the way to get out of that, is definitely not by having successive waves of punitive tariffs, which will not solve the problem.

Protectionism, as implemented under the American System of economy of Alexander Hamilton, was developed against the British Empire. But China is not your typical free trade country; China is not suppressing the wages of its population—to the contrary, they have lifted 800 million people out of poverty—that's not exactly a free trade characteristic—and they are sharing the most advanced technologies with the developing countries to help them overcome their underdevelopment as quickly as possible, by leapfrogging to the highest technologies. China's technology sharing policy is not a free trade policy.

Given the fact that President Trump has a very good relationship with President Xi, whom he continuously calls "my very good friend," I hope that the remaining time before the United States imposes a punitive level of 10% tariff on $200 billion of Chinese imports, that a

Xinhua/Pang Xinglei

Xi Jinping, President of China, addressing the eighth ministerial meeting of the China-Arab States Cooperative Forum in Beijing, China, July 10, 2018.

solution can be negotiated, by increasing trade as through joint ventures in third countries, which is what China's Prime Minister Li Keqiang has proposed.

I have not yet seen any discussion about the need for a New Bretton Woods explicitly. The Schiller Institute exists, to again and again precisely present such highly-needed solutions, and point to strategic matters that are absolutely crucial. I think that the inclination to create a sound banking system is evident in China's actions to create the Asian Infrastructure Investment Bank (AIIB), the New Silk Road Fund, and the Maritime Silk Road Fund. At the summit with the Arab nations, China just created a $20 billion fund for the reconstruction of Southwest Asia. Some of the headlines I read this morning indicated that China is extending the New Silk Road into Southwest Asia to reconstruct Yemen, Syria, Lebanon, and Jordan. That is what we have been proposing for many years.

So I think this is a very good thing, but we need to address this question of the New Bretton Woods the way my husband had proposed it many years ago. It's now more urgent than ever.

Schlanger: For people who want to be knowledgeable about this, we now have on the newparadigm.schillerinstitute.com website, all four panels from our June 30-July 1 conference, where these issues were discussed by people from Russia, China, from Africa, from Europe and the United States. I would like to get your thinking about the presentation by Vladimir Morozov, a speaker at the conference from Russia, who talked about the difference between a "multipolar" and "multilateral" approach to international relations. To what extent is this kind of discussion important in your view? You've been outspoken about the need to put an end to geopolitics, and I think the multipolar conception is part of a geopolitical formulation.

Zepp-LaRouche: Oh, yes. You can see this in the European Union, which claims that it is necessary to increase European integration to fend off alleged threats coming from Russia, China, or even the United States for that matter. That *is* geopolitics, and that is exactly what creates the potential for conflicts. The other approach is the New Paradigm and a new set of international relations as proposed by Xi Jinping—the idea of a "community of a shared future for mankind." That idea is one of *multilateral* relationships among sovereign nations, in which sovereign nations are united to advance the common aims of mankind, which advances all the different nations and groups of nations in the interest of all of humanity.

This is a very big difference. Looking at the long arc of history, it is clear that if we do not overcome geopolitics that the geopolitical view of a *multipolar* world could lead—and probably would lead in the short term—to the extinction of civilization. It is the nature of weapons that once you have them, you use them. In the age of nuclear weapons, I think conflict resolution through war should absolutely be forbidden, as should be evident to everyone, because of the consequences of such a war. The idea of a New Paradigm, of a new set of relations in which each nation respects the sovereignty of the others, in which each nation takes into account the idea of the mutual benefit of the other—this was the basis of the Peace of Westphalia, the basis for the UN Charter, and it was also the basis of the Human Rights Declaration of 1948.

We need a deeper discussion about the ontological conceptions underlying the international order, for it to function, and not just set one interest against the other in a rather mechanistic way. We have to address the deeper issues in each culture which allow all cultures to work together for a higher purpose.

Proposal for a Post-Colonial Era

Schlanger: You had a unique experience this last week in Paris: You were invited to address the Institut Mandela conference , in which you were able to put forward your proposal for how to address, not just the refu-

Test run of Ethiopia-Dijbouti railway in October 2016.

Highway project constructed by the China Road and Bridge Corporation, in Lome, Togo, 2014.

Nairobi Eastern & Northern Bypass constructed by the China Road and Bridge Corporation in Nairobi, Kenya, 2012.

gee crisis but for ending once and for all the post-colonial era. Tell us a little bit about the conference in Paris.

Zepp-LaRouche: This was a development based on my proposal to use the Singapore model for a crash program for the development of Africa, as the only human way to address this issue. In Europe, while the total number of refugees has gone down massively—so far this year, there have been only 43,000, as compared to one million in 2015. Nevertheless, the number of people drowning in the Mediterranean is increasing! There were more than 12,000 people who officially have drowned since 2014, I think, and that is probably not the total number, because not everybody who has drowned is accounted for.

I made my proposal, which we discussed last week, that the very successful Singapore summit between President Trump and President Kim Jong-un, should be used to turn a hopeless situation, or an almost hopeless and dangerous situation, into its opposite, by taking up the many proposals of China to work together with the Western nations in crash development programs in Africa. The Schiller Institute has produced many reports, the World Land-Bridge reports I and II, and *Extending the New Silk Road into West Asia and Africa*.

We have provided blueprints for the comprehensive development of all of Africa—ports, roads, highways, fast train systems, waterways, power production and distribution—as an integrated infrastructure program. I proposed in my "Singapore Model" idea, that once the heads of state of Africa, or those countries that want to do it, were to agree with European nations and China, and then invite Japan and India—you could start building such infrastructure everywhere all at once. You don't need to be restricted to laying one kilometer after the other of a fast train system in one area, before moving on to another. Once you agree on a comprehensive transport plan, you can start building, with the cooperation of several countries, in many nations at the same time, knowing each piece will fit together in the general plan, therefore allowing such construction to occur at an accelerated pace—a "crash" approach

My presentation of this basic idea at the Institut Mandela conference—at which there were many ambassadors and other institutional people from Africa—was extremely well received, for two reasons: The refugee crisis is on everybody's mind; but more importantly, there is a completely new sense of optimism in African countries. The New Silk Road Spirit has transformed the very idea of what can be done to reach, in the short term, a middle-class society. For example, the representative from the embassy of Ghana at that conference gave a very powerful speech, showing how Ghana is developing a middle class by not depending on merely exporting raw materials as such but more and more producing semi-finished products and finished products for export, and in that way lifting the productivity of Ghana's entire population. This is actually easy to do, once a government focuses on that approach, and having the kick start involvement of China, which has helped many countries in Africa.

The fact that there is now a peace process between Djibouti, Eritrea, and Ethiopia, is very much a cause for optimism. The new 750 km railway between Djibouti and Addis Ababa has now been functioning for several months, helping to create an environment where a relationship which was historically very difficult is now being transformed, and cooperation is now taking place.

This is obviously very important, because only 40 km across the Red Sea from Eritrea is Yemen, which is in a dire condition, suffering the worst humanitarian crisis on the planet. These are all concerns, but if the New Silk Road is extended into West Asia, and you have development in Africa, there is actually hope that eventually all of these problems can be solved.

So, I think there is right now, in many countries in the world—as a matter of fact, in almost all countries, with few exceptions—there is a complete spirit of change, of historic opportunity, of strategic realignments leading to a much better condition. There is reason for optimism that we can tackle these problems despite the fact that challenges naturally remain very big.

Schlanger: One analyst I speak with periodically made the point that while we're talking about a global insurgency or an awakening, it's not so much just an awakening to the fact that there's some "bad guys" out there—and people are beginning to pick up on especially the British—but that there's a solution; that what you call the New Silk Road Spirit is contagious, it's catching, and it is spreading. You gave me some examples earlier today. That spirit is even spreading into the usually—how can you describe it?—the German media: *Handelsblatt*, for example, published an article about what Germany could learn from China. So I assume you're even hopeful that this New Silk Road Spirit of the Singapore model could infect more and more Germans?

A Global Insurgency

Zepp-LaRouche: Well, you know, China is now doing everything which used to be German virtues, which Germany has unfortunately abandoned for the time being: Industriousness, reliability, punctuality, all of these things are now happening in China, and therefore, if *Handelsblatt* comes to the conclusion that China is doing something right, and then says what Germany could learn from China in terms of its industrial policy, I think it is quite interesting. The argument of this article says that Germany should pick certain areas of expertise in which Germans can be world leaders.

And Germany is, indeed about to lose that. For example, when a country wants to have a comprehensive infrastructure program, Germany has lost the ability to do these things in a grand style. Germany can obviously still supply many aspects, there are many so-called "hidden champions" in the German Mittelstand (high technology small and medium enterprises), which naturally are a treasure and very important. The idea that somehow the "free market" determines everything, is false. In reality, the European Central Bank (ECB) or other central banks and other powerful financial institutions rig those markets. I think the state needs to play a stronger role in the economy. I think a country has the right to set its priorities in terms of R&D development, in terms of where the future of industry should go. I'm optimistic, and this is why the Schiller Institute conducts conferences, not only in Germany but in many other countries, to bring this alternative to the table. I think this idea is beginning to bear fruit.

The Potential for a Better World

Schlanger: Helga, I know we've said a few things about the upcoming Trump and Putin summit. But just because of its importance, maybe in a final comment, could you say a little bit more about the potential, what areas they should focus on? Not the specifics so much, but for example, the sanctions issue is going to be taken up. What does it mean for the world that Trump and Putin will be meeting?

Zepp-LaRouche: The geopolitical manipulation of the world as we have seen it, by such things as fake news leading to military strikes against supposed chemical weapons use; or the fake news of a use of chemical weapons in Syria in order to disrupt the meeting between China and the United States; or Russiagate, which has now absolutely turned into "Muellergate." All of these things are happening, because—with a collaboration between the United States, Russia, China, with India now moving clearly closer, with Japan coming into this combination—the possibility to manipulate, in the typical British Empire way, to ally with the weakest against the stronger, or to play one side against the other, and have factions in each country, all of this will go out of the window.

President Putin has clearly managed to come back as a world player, who has demonstrated through his intervention in Syria that there is no solution to the Middle East crisis without the cooperation of Russia; that you cannot address international terrorism without working with Russia and China; and also the pending danger of a financial crisis. All these absolutely crucial issues could be solved were the adversarial relationship between the United States and Russia to disappear. There is now a very deep strategic partnership between Russia and China. Many other countries are realigning. For example, Japan has undergone a tremendous reset of its policy with respect to Russia, but also recently with respect to working with the New Silk Road.

So I think the potential is there that eventually most countries of the world will say, "It is much better to work together for the common interests of mankind, such as joint space exploration, discovering more about the unknown principles of our physical universe, developing human settlements on the Moon, having joint Mars missions and other joint space missions; for example, to defend the planet against the danger of asteroids and comets; and carry out earthquake research together, or similar crash programs. Were the nations to work together instead of against each other, the vast amounts of social capital currently wasted in the military sector could be re-directed into crash programs and projects which would make the lives of people better, such as curing cancer, and other now incurable diseases; by also developing space medicine, and connecting everybody even in the most remote areas of the world to a medical system which could save many, many lives. There are so many beautiful things we could do!

I'm Very Optimistic

And I'm very optimistic that we have a couple of leaders who are quite different in character—they're not all the same, they're not all of one kind—but I think you have a philosopher-king as the President of China—that's my deepest conviction; you have an excellent strategist in the person of Putin; and you have a person who has been courageous in upsetting a neo-liberal system which, after all, was responsible for many wars which, if you count the people who were killed in wars based on lies conducted by the Bush and Obama Administrations,— I think people forget that it is a good thing that Trump was able to upset this very powerful apparatus, and he has the inclination to try to improve the relationship with Russia and China.

And despite the fact that he sometimes says things which I have to say I disagree with, nevertheless, I have stuck my neck out early on by saying, if Trump succeeds in getting a good relationship between Russia and China and the United States, he will go down as one of the great Presidents of American history; I think that potential absolutely still exists. I really think we are in an incredible period, and those politicians who scream against everything that Putin is doing, or against China, the "big dictatorship," or Trump, the horrible "erratic" and whatnot—all of these people should think, because these are not the important things. What is important is that we move our planet and our civilization into a safe period, and establish peace on the planet, based on the development of all nations.

And I think that is what the nature of man says: The human species is the only creative species known so far, and we should be able to organize our relations among ourselves to have a truly sustainable development, which means growth, which means developments, which means continuous discoveries of more fundamental physical principles of our universe, and to grow up as a civilization.

Schlanger: By the time we reconvene next week, the Trump-Putin summit will have taken place, and I'm sure people will be very interested in hearing your analysis of what happened.

So Helga, thank you very much, and we'll see you next week!

Zepp-LaRouche: Yes, until next week.

II. Ideas as a Physical Force

THE OPIOID EPIDEMIC

An Assault on the Human Creative Personality

by Hector Villarreal

This is an edited transcript of a presentation given by Hector Villarreal on June 23, 2018, to a Schiller Institute meeting in Detroit, Michigan.

I want to address the opioid epidemic and the fight around the legalization of drugs from the standpoint of Lyndon LaRouche's economics, and his concept of human culture. I want to start by reading a quote from our pamphlet, "America's Future on the New Silk Road":

> Every infant born in any part of the world, has the potential for the development of his or her own mental powers to the level sufficient for a direct, competent use of modern technology. It is that potential development which is the only source of wealth.
>
> *—Lyndon H. LaRouche*

There is a hospital in Huntington, West Virginia, the Cabell Huntington Hospital, in which 1 in 10 babies born there is born addicted to some type of drug. In this economically devastated region of the country, that rate of babies born addicted is 15 times the national average.

In Ohio, the epicenter of the opioid crisis, the number of heroin overdoses rose 20% between the years 2015 and 2016. This is just in Ohio. Over the last seven years, the Public Children Services Association of Ohio (PCSAO) reported a 19% increase in the number of children taken into custody, due largely to the parents' addiction to heroin and painkillers. According to an article recently published in *The Hill*, over the

Cabell Huntington Hospital in 2006.

last four years, the number of children being brought into foster care due to drug-addicted parents has increased upwards of 30% nationwide.

So, the legalization of illicit drugs, the monetary benefit from them, or even the mere tolerance of them is a crime against humanity, whether that be cocaine, marijuana, or others mind-numbing drugs. When taken from the highest epistemological standpoint—and that is the standpoint of Mr. LaRouche's economics—and from the standpoint of the value of each human mind, such a crime against humanity must not be tolerated.

That may sound radical to some people, but that's what it is. In fact, America from its inception demonstrated this very idea. And China is demonstrating it right now. So, if this first quote I read by Mr. LaRouche is truthful, then the arguments for such legalization or toleration of drugs will dissipate.

Let me just re-read that first quote again with another, prefatory quote:

We hold these truths to be self evident, that all men are created equal.

Every infant born in any part of the world, has the potential for the development of his or her own mental powers to the level sufficient for a direct, competent use of modern technology. It is that potential development which is the only source of wealth.

Therefore, to accept the use of mind-altering illicit drugs is to diminish your workforce, diminish its skill level and ability to operate machinery, and all other kinds of actually human labor. Even more important is the diminishment of each person's creative potential to make new discoveries, to assimilate those discoveries and to transfer them to future generations, which Mr. LaRouche would say is the substance of immortality, the role of a nation-state.

It is that creative identity of mankind which was intended to be destroyed with the paradigm shift of the 1960s. The assassinations of the Kennedy brothers, Martin Luther King and Malcolm X, the deindustrialization policy and the drug policy were actually all one process, aimed at destroying that creative capability of the American people. We've documented thoroughly that this operation was carried out by high-level thinkers within the British Empire, as well as their allies within the CIA and FBI. Some of these facts are actually well known. I won't go into detail in this presentation; I just want to highlight one quote from one of the British architects of the Sex, Drugs and Rock n' Roll counterculture.

This is what he said to a medical group in San Francisco, in the early 1960s:

> There will be, in the next generation or so, a pharmacological method of making people love their servitude, and producing a dictatorship without

public domain: New York World-Telegram and Sun/*Albertain Walter*

Dr. Martin Luther King, Jr. presenting his book, Why We Can't Wait, *at a press conference on June 8, 1964.*

tears, so to speak, producing a kind of painless concentration camp for entire societies, so that people will in fact have their liberties taken away from them, but will rather enjoy it, because they will be distracted from any desire to rebel by propaganda or brainwashing, or brainwashing enhanced by pharmacological methods. And this seems to be the final revolution.

> —*Aldous Huxley*

The drug issue, as I'm trying to pose it here, is not an issue of drugs, but rather culture. In as few words as possible, we can describe culture as how society deals with problems. How does it deal with injustice? Does it disassociate itself? Does it dive into the escapism of drugs or entertainment? Does it seek pleasure and avoid pain? Or, does it confront problems directly and attempt to overcome them creatively? In other words, is it a scientific approach?

I want to give an example in American culture, a culture that was once steeped in classical culture. It was not perfect then, but it did exist and it was not what we have now.

In 1963 Martin Luther King and the Southern Christian Leadership Council were on a campaign to end segregation and racial injustice. Martin Luther King was invited to Birmingham because Birmingham was the most racially segregated city in the United States. The objective was to bring national attention to that fact through the use of nonviolent direct action. King and about fifty others were arrested the day of the rally for failure to have a permit. You may think that he drew approval and praise. In fact, he drew criticism. He drew criticism from many of the local Jewish and Christian leaders. He was attacked as an outside agitator, whose actions were unwise and untimely. He was notified of this criticism as he sat in a Birmingham jail, and he penned his famous letter there. I want to read a small section of his response:

Poor People's March in Washington, D.C. on June 18, 1968.

U.S. News & World Report/Library of Congress

You may well ask, "Why direct action? Why sit-ins, marches, etc.? Isn't negotiation a better path?" You are exactly right in your call for negotiation. Indeed, this is the purpose of direct action. Nonviolent direct action seeks to create such a crisis and establish such creative tension that a community that has constantly refused to negotiate is forced to confront the issue. It seeks so to dramatize the issue that it can no longer be ignored. I just referred to the creation of tension as a part of the work of the nonviolent resister. This may sound rather shocking. But I must confess that I am not afraid of the word tension. I have earnestly worked and preached against violent tension, but there is a type of constructive nonviolent tension that is necessary for growth. Just as Socrates felt that it was necessary to create a tension in the mind so that individuals could rise from the bondage of myths and half-truths to the unfettered realm of creative analysis and objective appraisal, we must see the need of having nonviolent gadflies to create the kind of tension in society that will help men rise from the dark depths of preju-dice and racism to the majestic heights of understanding and brotherhood.

—*Martin Luther King*

King did not stop at civil rights, but he went beyond what others were willing to do and continued his fight for economic justice for all, for not just people in the South but for the country and the entire world. It was called the Poor People's Campaign. Another champion of economic justice, Robert Kennedy, was assassinated—along with King—within a two month period in 1968. The country then collapsed into deep cultural pessimism and drug use, which were being flooded into the country.

This crisis of drugs, deindustrialization, and pessimism is today all-pervasive. This is what Sam Quinones notes in his book *Dreamland*: that the opioid epidemic leaves out no demographic, young, old, rich or poor, white or black. Everyone here should have received a copy of the *Dreamland* book review we published in *EIR;* it is a very good summary of the book. Quinones details the campaign of Big Pharma, which lied to the public and medical community, saying that these opiate painkillers were not addictive. They started their campaign by corrupting large sections of the medical community in order to get the over-prescription of opioids accepted, and then began marketing these highly-addictive drugs in areas that had been destroyed economically, because the people there were the most vulnerable. This laid the basis for the epidemic.

It's an interesting story, which shows how these large, prestigious pharmaceutical companies converged on the Midwest, together with the brutal Mexican cartels, in order to infect America's heartland. It's a riveting story, but I want to point out the insights that Mr. Quinones developed in writing the book. He notes that important values have been lost in this

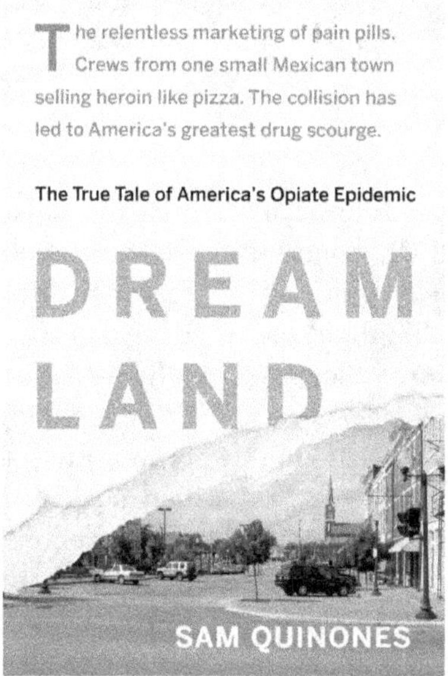

process. Those values being a sense of productiveness, the value of creative participation in strengthening community and government, and the ability to work through stress and pain for the sake of something better for future generations.

Mr. Quinones testified on this very issue before the Senate Health, Education, Labor and Pensions Committee this last January. He presented his findings in the book and provided his solution. I want to end with what he said there.

View this as an opportunity to revive those regions hammered by globalization and free trade. The roots of our national epidemic of narcotic addiction lie there, while the epidemic itself, in turn, stands in the way of their revival.

Dr. Werner Von Braun (left) explains the Saturn system to President John F. Kennedy at Cape Canaveral in 1963.

I believe American history offers us two templates for actions, from which you might take guidance and inspiration. The first is the Marshall Plan to rebuild Europe after World War II. The second is our space program. Each involved the government and the private sector acting in concert over many years, bringing money, brains, energy, and of course long-term focus to bear. Each achieved an unalloyed good for our country; although they were both things that seemed, at first blush, far beyond our own, short-term self interest.

The Marshall plan was about building up ravaged regions to allow them to function independently…. it allowed reborn countries to prosper and contribute to the world again. A Marshall Plan for American recovery might focus on rebuilding those regions that have been caught in dependence on dope, and ravaged by economic devastation, to contain the viral spread of addiction.

Through our space program we were inspired as a people, to spend years and dollars, all to achieve something no previous generation ever thought possible. We ended up far beyond the Moon. The spillover in economic benefit, increase in knowledge, and simple human inspiration, is beyond calculation.

It seems to me that we might profitably apply these examples—the Marshall Plan, and the space program—to regions of forgotten Americans where this addiction problem began. Let's do it, not because it is easy, but as JFK said, because it is hard; because that's what Americans do, and have always done, at their greatest.

Like our space program, I believe such an effort will have to last for years to be effective, focused far beyond the immediate goal of drug addiction, and on the more profound problems of community destruction and the hollowing-out of stretches of this country.

It offers an opportunity to reinvest in areas that need it most, a chance to inspire us as Americans again, to something great…. Do not miss this opportunity. It does not come around often…. You will be remembered for acting, when acting was not easy to do.

Thank you.

You're Human! Do You Know What That Means?

by Robert Ingraham

IV.—The Mind Masters the Biosphere

July 10—The question posed to the reader here is to reflect on one's own mind. Examine the manner in which you make decisions, how you ascertain the truth or falsehood of a proposition, or how you go about verifying new insights and discoveries. In this series, we have already discussed several of the important scientific and technological discoveries accomplished by the human species. In this chapter we shall discuss more of these. Yet, each of these breakthroughs was accomplished by a single individual. This is the nature of creativity, and it is the origin of all human progress: an individual, alone, reflecting on his or her own beliefs, uncompromisingly challenging the veracity of what one holds to be true.

The human mind—where our soul, our sense of identity resides—is always in a dialogue with itself.

"Along the River During the Qingming Festival," by Zhang Zeduan (12th Century).

The nature of that dialogue and the courage with which it is conducted will determine one's ability to arrive at truthful conclusions concerning the nature of the universe and the human identity. This defines the relationship between the creative capacity of the human mind and the creative nature of the universe. It is the human mind examining itself and striving for new lawful insights into universal principles which creates the only pathway to wisdom.

As has already been stated in earlier parts of this report, Lyndon LaRouche has specified the relative health of a physical-economic system—i.e., any specific form of human culture, properly defined—as to be found in an anti-entropic increase in the rate of growth in that culture's *potential relative population density*. However, let us be precisely clear about this: the phrase "potential relative population density" is not a number, a ratio, a goal, nor a statistic. Rather, an anti-entropic increase in a society's ability to support—and to require—a growing population defines the increasing *noëtic* energy of human culture, the potential that humanity possesses for further advancement, and an anti-entropic increase in Man's power over the biosphere. All of this is born inside of the individual human mind. This potential is what exists within your own mind.

Such cognitively-driven economic progress requires revolutions in science, technology, industry and all other forms of physical production—scientific and technological "leaps" which make an anti-entropic increase in humanity's power possible.

What we are looking at here is mankind taking increasing mastery over all biological and inorganic processes on the planet Earth—bending the resources of the planet to serve the increasingly advanced and beautiful mission of humanity. This defines actual willful human evolution.

In this portion of our inquiry, we shall look at China, and the way in which China, for most of the last three millennia, has spearheaded the creative breakthroughs that sparked human advancement. This is not to say that "all good things came from China." In science, industry and astronomy many discoveries came from India, particularly in the earliest phases of human civilization. Later, after 700 AD, the Arab and Islamic world made great contributions.[1] Yet, in China

we see a clear picture of how a lawful understanding of the human identity together with great progress in the physical sciences advanced hand-in-hand. And, again, we see the courage of key individuals in challenging themselves, examining the basis for their own beliefs, and testing hypotheses as to the principles which underlie creation.

Ancient Chinese bronze bell, from c.500-450 BC, on exhibit at the Freer Gallery of Art, Washington, D.C.

New Economic Platforms for Humanity

Below is a timeline. The purpose for its inclusion here is straightforward: to provide a bare-bones picture of Chinese advances which led humanity into the future.

- Before 1,000 BC—The widespread use of coal to smelt copper.
- 770-476 BC—The development of the blast furnace. This allowed the heating of ore above its melting point, in order to produce cast iron. Cast iron production would not enter Europe until 1380 AD, two millennia later.
- 550 BC—Construction of the first section of the Grand Canal. Today, almost 2,600 years later, the 1,104-mile Grand Canal is still the longest man-made waterway in the world.

---

1. One example: As early as the Sixth Century, India developed very high quality "ukku" (or "wootz") steel. The famous "Damascus steel" was the forged steel used for the blades of swords smithed in the Near East from ingots of wootz steel from India.

China's Beijing-Hangzhou (Grand) Canal, the longest and oldest canal in the world.

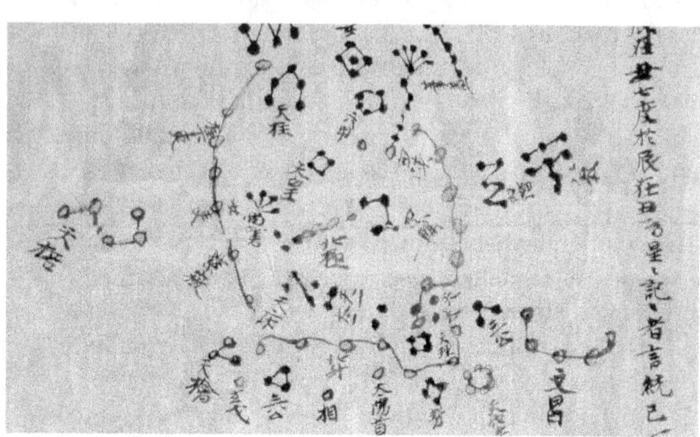

Star map of the celestial sphere, by Su Song (AD 1020-1101).

HAN DYNASTY (Western Han, 202 BC-9 AD; Eastern Han, 23-220 AD)

- 200 BC—The invention of steel, using what became known in the West (2,000 years later) as the Bessemer process. They converted cast iron into steel, by blowing air—through bellows—on the molten metal, which reduced the carbon content.
- 119 BC—The Han Dynasty took control of all cast-iron manufacture to ensure widely available, high-quality tools and implements. These included plowshares, hoes, axes, chisels, saws, etc. These superior tools led to a substantial advance in productivity throughout the entire economy.
- 100 BC—The earliest Chinese development of the armillary sphere, enabling the measurement of the north polar distance.[2]
- 60 BC—Invention of the first celestial globe by Geng Shou-chang.
- 25-50 AD—The use of waterwheels to operate the bellows of a blast furnace to make pig iron, and the cupola furnace to make cast iron. This process was invented by Du Shi.
- 50 AD (or earlier)—The invention of the rudder, which greatly enhanced the systematic exploration of the oceans. The rudder first appeared in Europe in 1180 AD.

- 100 AD—Mapping the ecliptic to an armillary sphere (showing the Earth's inclination) by Zhang Heng.
- 100 AD—Development of first "star map" by Zhang Heng, containing 2,500 stars and 100 constellations.
- 105 AD—Invention of paper. This aided in the transmission of knowledge throughout China.
- 150 AD—First recorded ocean voyage of a Chinese Junk, the most advanced sea-going ship on Earth until the emergence of the carrack in Renaissance Europe 1,300 years later.
- 185 AD—First recorded observation of a supernova, in the direction of Alpha Centauri, between the constellations Circinus and Centaurus. It remained visible in the night sky for eight months.

- 258 AD—The harnessing of water power for industrial purposes, including the introduction of water driven piston-rods, drive-belts and forge-hammers, vastly increasing the amount of work that could be performed per capita, from iron work, to grinding grain. Arrived in Europe in the 12th and 13th centuries.
- 400 AD—Perfection of the manufacture of steel, using coal as a high-temperature fuel, good refractory clays for the blast furnace walls, and phosphorus to reduce the temperature at which iron melts.
- 800-850 AD—First use of coke for heating and cooking. This led to the widespread use of coke in the iron industry.

---

2. The first armillary sphere was invented by the Greek astronomer Eratosthenes in 255 BC, during the period before Platonic/Hellenic culture was snuffed out by the rise of the Roman empire.

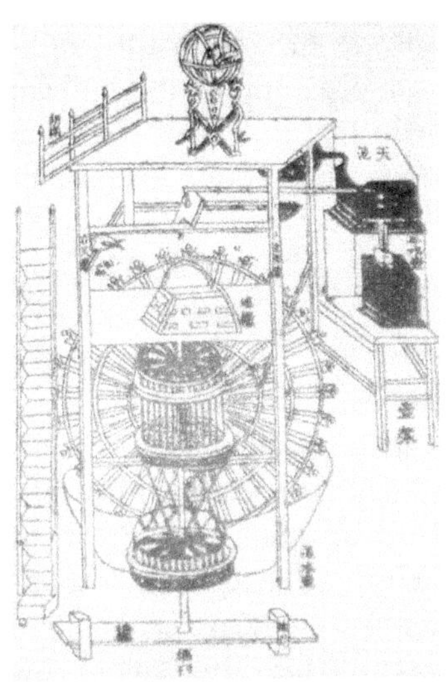

Clock tower diagram from Su Song's book of 1092.

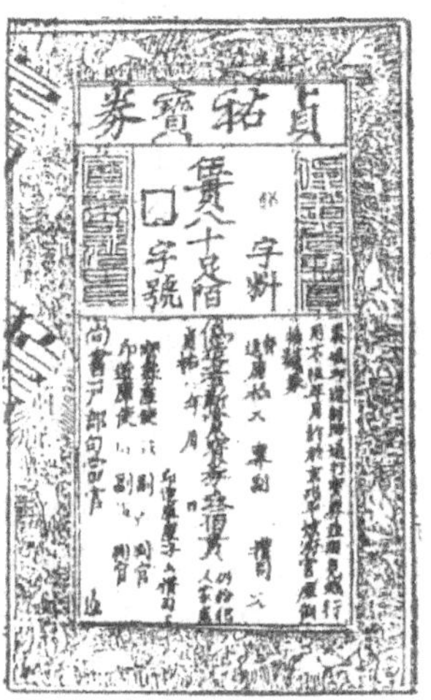

Copper plate for making paper money, from Jin Dynasty (AD 1115-1234).

Painting of Suzhou sailing vessels moored on the Grand Canal by Xu Yang (active c.1750-1776).

SONG DYNASTY (960-1279 AD)

- 1000 AD—Invention of movable type for printing by Bi Sheng.
- 1000-1279—The construction of huge astronomical observatories, resulting in a series of highly accurate star-maps.
- 1054 AD—Chinese astronomers observe and record the supernova which created the Crab Nebula.
- 1070 AD—Invention of the dry-dock to repair sea-going ships.
- 1100 AD—Invention of the mariner's compass by Shen Kuo, as well as the discovery and means of measuring one's true meridian (longitude) by measuring the distance between the pole star and true north as defined by Earth's axis of rotation. These discoveries were brought into Europe and were crucial to the European voyages of discovery in the 15th Century.
- 1100 AD—Song China was producing 127,000 tons of iron per year.[3] Waterwheels, windmills, advanced designs of bellows, and the use of bituminous coke[4] in industrial processes all became widespread. Great advances were made in shipbuilding and navigation, and it was under the Song, that paper currency was introduced and used to finance the nation's physical economic development. During the Song Dynasty, per capita iron output rose sixfold, and the population of China doubled in size during the 11th Century.

---

3. By comparison, in 1788, England's production of iron was around 50,000 tons.

4. Coal became a universal source of energy for virtually all purposes in China, something which would not be seen in Europe until the 18th and 19th centuries.

The Mind Moves the Universe

The list above describes two millennia of inventions, discoveries and actions through which mankind began to exert increasing control over the physical evolution of our planet and established an upward development of the human species. In military terms, a cognitive beachhead was seized, for the deployment of a permanent human role within the galaxy. Many of these Chinese discoveries and inventions made their way into Europe, the Islamic world, and other regions, particularly after the final collapse of the Roman Empire in the west.

If one looks at one of the individuals mentioned above, Zhang Heng, the scope and intent of this Chinese cognitive offensive begins to come into focus.

Zhang Heng (78-139 AD), was an astronomer, mathematician, scientist, engineer, geographer, cartographer, artist and poet who lived during the Han dynasty. Zhang invented

A 1955 Chinese postage stamp depicting Zhang Heng (78-139 AD), Han Dynasty scientist and statesman.

the world's first water-powered armillary sphere to assist astronomical observation; he invented the world's first seismoscope, which discerned the direction of an earthquake 500 km away; he postulated the idea of the

Earth's ecliptic (the apparent path that the Sun follows over the Earth), calculating the Earth's axial tilt in relation to the ecliptic at 26°5′ (which is just 3° off the modern measurement of 23°27′). In his treatise *Ling Xian* (Mystical Laws), Zhang describes the nature of both solar and lunar eclipses, and he identifies both that the Moon moves around the Earth and that it is an illuminated body, i.e., that it reflects light from the Sun.

Zhang was part of a much larger scientific renaissance during the Han Dynasty; he was associated with a group of similar scholars, including the mathematician and calligrapher Cui Yuan (78-143 AD), the philosophical commentator Ma Rong (79-166), and the philosopher Wang Fu (78-163 AD), among others. The common thread which links these individuals together is that they were all leading Confucian scholars.

Earlier, during the reign of the Emperor Wu of Han (157-87 BC), the teachings of Confucius (551-479 BC) were adopted as the official state philosophy, and all government officials and members of the Han court were required to study and pass examinations in the teaching of Confucius. Despite many later dark periods of moral and economic decline in China, this Confucian outlook within Chinese culture has persisted to the present day, and if one looks at the two greatest cultural renaissances in subsequent Chinese history—the Song dynasty (960-1279 AD) and the present-day Belt and Road Initiative of President Xi Jinping—both are associated with a deliberate and willful effort to revive and advance the Confucian outlook.

Emperor Wu of Han (ruled from 141-87 BC).

In 1925, Sun Yat Sen, the founder of modern China, told an interviewer that his lifelong efforts toward effecting revolutionary change in China were all based on "a development and continuation of the ancient Chinese doctrines of Confucius." As a child, Sun read *The Great Learning*, the *Doctrine of the Mean*, the *Confucian Analects*, and the *Works of Mencius*—known collectively as the Four Books—as well as the Five Classics, including the *Spring and Autumn Annals*. It is often stated that Sun's "Three Principles of the People"—and particularly the third Principle, the "People's Livelihood" (*min sheng*)—were greatly influenced by the moral and political outlook of Abraham Lincoln, and there is truth in that assertion. Yet, Sun himself stated that the outlook upon which his revolutionary program was based—including his plans for the industrialization of China—was all to be found in Confucius and Mencius.

Sun would quote from Mencius, "If the people have a sure livelihood, they will have a fixed heart. If they have not a sure livelihood, they have not a fixed heart. And if they have not a fixed heart, there is nothing they will not do in the way of self-abandonment, of moral deflection, of depravity, and of wild license." This was the same Sun who, in the final months of his life, urged his young protégé Chiang Kai-shek to study the Confucian classics.

A Universe Based on Principle

A beautiful investigation into Confucian philosophy has recently been supplied by *EIR*, in the form of an article, "Toward the Ecumenical Unity of East and West: Confucianism, Christianity, and the Peace of Faith," by Michael Billington. No attempt will be made here to investigate in depth what Billington reports in that and others of his works.[5] We shall simply emphasize that the Confucian insistence that a universal human identity is based upon cognitive reason—and that this creative feature of the human identity is eternally linked to the moral virtue of what we in the West call *agapē*—has infused much of Chinese culture for more than 2,000 years, and it has supplied a *noëtic* power to the human species that has led the forward advance of human civilization throughout most of recorded history.

The heart of Confucianism is the principle of *Ren* (sometimes spelled *Jen*). One of the Confucian *Four Virtues*, *Ren* is often referred to as "benevolence," but this misses the full coherence of Ren with the Western term *agapē*—i.e., love of truth, love of the Creator, love

<hr>

5. See also Billington's "The Taoist Perversion of Twentieth-Century Science," *Fidelio*, Fall, 1994, and "Toward the Ecumenical Unity of East and West," *Fidelio*, Summer, 1993.

of the creation, love of fellow man. The other three Virtues are Righteousness, Propriety (meaning behavior which benefits oneself and society), and Wisdom. All of these Virtues involve willful human action: *Ren* governs one's relations with others; Righteousness defines a morally sound character; Propriety defines one's actions as benefitting the Common Good; and Wisdom defines a development of one's cognitive abilities from whence all proper action flows. True Wisdom can only be approached through an investigation into the ordering of creation and Man's role within that creation.

Centuries later, during the Song Dynasty, Zhu Xi (1130-1200 AD) further advanced the precepts of Confucian learning. Zhu developed the concept of *Li* or Principle. He puts forward the idea of Universal Principle, a Principle which contains within it all of the *Four Virtues* as one whole, and he asserts that this Universal Principle, as an active Principle, is the governing Principle of all of creation. He goes further, identifying the individual *Li* which exists in all individual created things, and he posits that the individual *Li* both reflects and participates in the Universal *Li*.

It is this outlook, as developed by Confucius, Mencius, Zhu Xi and others, which Gottfried Leibniz called the "natural philosophy" or "natural theology" of the Chinese, seeing in it a reflection of his own work, as exemplified in the *Theodicy* and the *Monadology*. This defines a human identity of *noëtic* power, linked directly to the ongoing universal process of lawful creation.

Man and the Galaxy

Reaching far back into recorded history, and continuing into the 21st Century with modern China's increasing role in space exploration, great individuals from within Chinese culture have always looked to the stars to discover the true nature of Man's role in the galaxy. During the Song Dynasty (960-1279), one of the key scientific leaders was Shen Kuo (1031-1095), an astronomer, meteorologist, geologist, botanist, archaeologist, cartographer, hydraulic engineer, and mathematician. He was also a diplomat, finance minister, poet and musician. He served as the head of the Imperial Department of Astronomy in the Song court.

Dr. Sun Yat-sen, founding father of the Republic of China, in London in 1911.

Shen Kuo was a devout student of the works of Mencius (372 BC-289 BC), and he authored a commentary on the philosophy of Mencius. In it, he emphasizes the importance of following what one knows to be a true path. He states that the heart and mind can never attain full knowledge of truth through mere sensory experience, but only through an examination of higher lawful principles. The truth can not be attained through merely studying "things," but through the discovery of new lawful principles which define the nature of all existence. Shen wrote of an autonomous inner authority— which exists in every human being— that forms the basis for one's inclination toward moral choices.

Shen authored a work of 507 essays, known today as the *Dream Pool Essays*. It is here that many of his scientific investigations are reproduced. He describes the magnetic needle compass, which would be used for navigation. He discusses the use of the drydock to repair sea-going ships. He describes the functioning of the newly invented canal pound lock. He describes the *camera obscura*, and he writes extensively about printing with movable type, recently invented by Bi Sheng (990-1051).

Experimenting with suspended magnetic needles, Shen discovered that the magnetic north was not the true geographical north, and he was able to calculate a precise measurement of the magnetic declination. Shen also charted the rotation of the polar star, which together with the use of the compass, revolutionized Chinese navigation practices. He also made improved designs of the armillary sphere, the gnomon and the sighting tube.

Together with his colleague Wei Pu, Shen initiated a five-year project to map the orbital paths of the Moon and the planets, involving daily observations, but this project was never completed. Based on his initial studies, Shen hypothesized that the planets have retrograde motion in their orbits. He also proposed the theory that heavenly bodies were spheres, based on his observations of the waxing and waning of the Moon. He supported the hypothesis, proposed earlier by Zhang Heng, that the Moon was reflective, rather than producing light itself.

Shen devised a geological hypothesis for land formation, based upon findings of inland marine fossils, knowledge of soil erosion, and the deposition of silt. He also put forward a theory of gradual climate change, after observing ancient petrified bamboos that were preserved in a dry northern habitat which would not support bamboo growth in his time.

The Song Economic Revolution

The era of the Song Dynasty was one of great human discovery and creation. At the center of it was the intervention of Zhu Xi (1130-1200 AD) and his admonition to "investigate the Principle in things to the utmost." Zhu insisted that a true understanding of Universal Principle (*Li*) was required to move China forward. As discussed above, Zhu's investigation into the relationship between Universal *Li* and individual *Li*, defined what we in the West

Zhu Xi, Confucian scholar in the Song Dynasty.

might call a Promethean Identity for every human individual. This led to an explosion of scientific and technological discoveries, with each discovery rapidly disseminated throughout China, made possible by the 10th Century invention of printing with movable type.

Zhu Xi served the Song Court for nine years, during which time he initiated numerous projects on water management, canal building and education. He established public granaries to provide a reliable source of food for all Chinese. He proposed recruiting poor and unemployed Chinese to build needed infrastructure.

One of the greatest accomplishments of this era was the agricultural revolution. This was accomplished not by bringing more land into cultivation, but by applying scientific discoveries to revolutionize food production. These included new hydraulic techniques and irrigation networks; new seed strains, to increase yields and enhance the capability for double cropping; improved methods of soil preparation, utilizing fertilizers and tools; and a vast network of roads and canals. All of this was greatly aided by Chinese advances in metallurgy and industrial production. By the Thirteenth Century, China possessed the most advanced agriculture in the world. Potential population density exploded.

As stated above, by 1100 AD China was producing 127,000 tons of iron per year. Other industrial, hydraulic, power and related technologies were the most ad-

vanced in the world. Internal and foreign trade boomed. Shipbuilding became a major industry, producing thousands of inland and seagoing ships. The mariner's compass, invented about 1119, led to the charting of the sea and advanced navigation techniques.

During the Song era, the population of China more than doubled, and Chinese breakthroughs in science and technology—breakthroughs which gave mankind increased power in the universe—radiated throughout all of the human species.

Saving Europe

We shall reserve our discussion of oligarchic empire for the next installment of this serial. Here, we shall simply note that, following the conclusion of the Roman Empire's Third Punic War in 146 BC and the assassination of the brothers Gracchi in 133 BC and 123 BC, respectively, Europe entered into a prolonged Dark Age, one which lasted for 1,500 years.

There were breakthroughs and advances—the reign of Charlemagne in Europe and the scientific contributions of the Islamic world being the greatest interventions—yet, for centuries Europe was held back and driven down by oligarchical rule. It was in China that human culture advanced and prospered.

Through the activity conducted along the Silk Road trading route, as well as the maritime trade of India and the Islamic world, many Chinese scientific and technological breakthroughs made their way to the West. Also, during the Song and other dynasties, numerous foreign scientists and entrepreneurs took up residence in China, with Muslim astronomers being of particular note. China was not isolated; it was not a "hidden" Shangri-La. Throughout all of these centuries, China led and contributed to a great Dialogue of Civilizations.

Many Chinese discoveries were transmitted into Europe. These would help sustain the people of Europe during very difficult times, and provide a scientific and technological reservoir, one to be drawn on, as Europe began to move forward in the 15th Century.

To be continued.

January 9, 2010

The Question Before Us

by Lyndon H. LaRouche, Jr.

The question addressed by the following presentation, is:

What are to be recommended for consideration as perspectives for what is (a) a truly, urgently needed four-power initiative on behalf of a mission-oriented process of transformation of the world's economic systems, (b) away from the presently ruinous effects of submission to an implicitly financially imperialist, global monetarist system, a virtual "new Tower of Babel," and, (c) toward an urgently needed, fixed-exchange-rate credit system of (d) mutually beneficial, global cooperation among peoples organized as a community of respectively sovereign nation-states.

This presumes the indispensable, included, practical measure of the included, (e) immediate application of the precedent provided as the principle of the Glass-Steagall reform which was introduced to the U.S.A. under U.S. President Franklin Roosevelt.

Which also means, once more, (f) the eradication of intrinsically pro-imperialist, monetary systems, by their replacement by (g) a system of sovereign national credit-systems configured in the formation of a long-term, fixed-exchange rate array of national credit-systems.

Since most of the nominal monetary-financial assets abroad presently, are loaded with an implicitly hyperinflationary accumulation of increasingly worthless "paper," an immediate change from a monetary system, to a fixed-exchange-rate credit system, is the only presently available hope for avoiding the plunge of the planet as a whole into a prolonged new dark age.

What is written on the current state of the British empire, is admittedly harsh, but must be stated as a truthful representation, without fear of any actual exaggeration respecting the current policies of practice of the present British Royal House. I have been careful, not to overlook the natural, national rights of the people of the United Kingdom, with whom I, after all, share a certain ancient ancestry.

On the Subject of a Four Great-Powers Initiative

The planet considered as a whole, is now hovering at the virtual brink of a world-wide, new dark age, which, if present trends in policy are permitted to continue, will become a condition comparable to, but far worse than that which Europe experienced during what is called the Fourteenth-century "New Dark Age."

The root of that threat has been the same British Empire which had organized every general catastrophe on this planet since the onset of that so-called "Seven Years War" of 1756-1763, a British Empire which, for example, had brought Adolf Hitler to power in Germany in 1933, but which had turned, in desperation, to the U.S.A. for help against its own former German puppet, Hitler, but only after the attacks leading to the Fall of France and the consequent threat to the British overseas empire itself. Churchill's Britain then pled for succor from the United States.

Then, once President Franklin Roosevelt had died, Britain turned around again, to relaunch what had been its long-ranging intention to bring down the United States, and to proceed toward Britain's aim of establishing a neo-Malthusian form of a single world empire, a virtual "New Tower of Babel," which is the core of that monarchy's immediate, present, wicked perspective.

The U.S.A. administration of President Barack Obama, a figure whose policies are cast in the likeness of a caricature of those of Britain's former Prime Min-

NASA/Pat Rawlings (SAIC)

An alliance of the four great powers would define a mission-oriented process of transformation of the world's economic systems. Immediately, this would mean unifying the world's railroads into a modern, global system. The next step would be the colonization of the Moon and then Mars. Shown: an artist's rendering of a rocket refueling in a Mars orbit, en route to Jupiter.

That wicked policy which was initiated under British Prime Minister Margaret Thatcher, and was done in concert with France's pro-British President of that time, François Mitterrand, and also with a complicit U.S. President George H.W. Bush, cleared the way for the broadly applied, deliberate destruction of the economy of not only what had become imperial Britain's traditional European target, Germany, that since the great economic reform under U.S. friend Chancellor Bismarck. This was a ruin intended for the systemically savage, "pacification, through brutality, of the weakened victim;" it embodied a program of economic destruction including virtually the entire region of the former Soviet Union and the Comecon, with the intended ruin of Germany, as of the nations of both the former Comecon and Russia. Such are the methods of triumphant predators, such as the British monarchy now, predators who sow, thus, the seeds of prolonged wars and kindred sorts of terrible convulsions.

The development of the so-called "Euro," a system which was set into motion by the initiative of those three powers of the 1989-1990 developments, Britain, France, and the 1989-1993 U.S.A. under President George H.W. Bush, has since resonated, in effects, to the point, that since the close of July 2007, the set of nations now included in the relevant Lisbon Treaty's crushing of the national sovereignties of the relevant victim-nations of continental Europe, has temporarily eliminated essential elements of national sovereignties from what had been, until then, the respectively sovereign states of western and central continental Europe.

What has been done to western and central Europe, under that reign by the monetarist oligarchy of London, is what is also intended, by London, to be done to the United States of America and every other nation of Europe, and of Asia, the extended Pacific-Indian oceans' regions, Africa, and the entirety of the Ameri-

ister Tony Blair, is serving, thus far, as the British puppet employed in the effort to bring down the U.S.A. by means of the Devil's own sort of virtual treason unloosed from within the current administration, an effort, nominally led by President Barack Obama, which, if successful, would clear the way to mopping-up Britain's other chief obstacles on this planet, such as Russia, China, and India, as if one at a time.

Thus, the present circumstances of global crisis, demand that we now, quickly address the subject of certain specific evils which had been brought upon Europe through a reorganization of the affairs of the planet which occurred two decades ago, a reorganization pursued through the overreaching bit of common action taken in the matter of London's prescribed conditions for the reunification, then, of what had been London's already traditional enemy, Germany, since Chancellor Bismarck's U.S.-modeled economic reforms.

These were the conditions set by a trio of Britain's Prime Minister Margaret Thatcher, by France's President Mitterrand, and, the assent to their actions by then U.S. President George H.W. Bush. Since that time, that action launched by those three, at that point in history, has become increasingly ruinous in its implications for both the present and the future of not only Europe, but, now, for the peoples of the planet as a whole.

The British attack on the sovereignty of nations is intended to reduce the planet to "the ruined likeness of an imperial form of a new Tower of Babel." Shown is Peter Bruegel the Elder's "The Tower of Babel" (1563).

nearly 7 billions persons, to less than 2, is an evil scheme, long associated with British Royal Consort Prince Philip, who is allied with the President Obama who is now operating in a manner suggestive of treason, behind the back of the people of the U.S.A., a policy of Prince Philip which represents the greatest evil loosed upon this planet today.

Meanwhile, since the time when the U.S. economy was plunged into a presently accelerating, global breakdown-crisis, since the close of July 2007, the greatest rate of increase of a presently suffocating mass of essentially fictitious financial capital, has overtaken the United States, while, with the advent of this present Year 2010, the U.S. Obama government has taken new measures which, if tolerated, will tend to throw the U.S.A. itself into an onrushing general breakdown-crisis of a quality whose consequence would be the already threatened plunge of the world economy as a whole, as by a planet-wide chain-reaction, into a condition akin to that experienced by Europe as its Fourteenth-Century "New Dark Age."

cas, too. "Divide and conquer," is the method of the British Foreign Office, operating now, under Queen Elizabeth II, through what is called "the British Commonwealth." She has attempted the use of that Commonwealth as a first line of imperial monetarist power, as this was to be seen in the evils expressed by the role of the Queen in the matter of the relevant efforts within the "Copenhagen summit."

The attack on the sovereignty of the U.S.A. now, through the current role of that virtual British royal puppet, U.S. President Obama, is typical of the effort, as since the evil done by Obama confederate and former British Prime Minister, Tony Blair, to reduce the planet as a whole to the ruined likeness of an imperial form of a new Tower of Babel.

It must be presently recognized as the leading issue of the most recent course of history, that the consent, by some nations, to the vicious impoverishment of some other nations, unleashes the threat of the ultimate impoverishment and ruin of all nations. We are morally obliged to act to remove the relevant present threat to this planet.

Thus, the mass-murderous partnership between the British monarchy and President Obama, which is intended to reduce the world's population, rapidly, from

I must affirm afresh, at this point, that, whereas, it might have appeared to some misguided nations, that they had benefitted from some relatively exceptional degree of useful economic growth during some part of the recent period, as all nations and peoples inhabit the same planet, to such an effect that all nations, to one degree or another, whether directly, or indirectly, have become, ultimately, the common victims of the global threat of a new, post-1989 form of what is practically a British imperial tyranny, called "globalization," over the planet and its peoples considered as a whole.

So, I must affirm the point, that the effects of the process of globalization, effects with the characteristics of a deep-going global "new malthusianism," which were set into motion in the terms dictated to Germany two decades ago, by the concerted action of Thatcher, Mitterrand, and Bush, are, presently, the source of the threat of a presently early arrival at the entry of the planet as a whole into a prolonged, global new dark age of all humanity. This is an effect which, if allowed to continue, even during the immediate months ahead, would soon unleash what the present British monarchy, and its accomplice, President Barack Obama, have explicitly intended to become the worst holocaust suffered by all humanity in the known, detailed political-economic history of mankind.

In such a process, the smaller and weaker nations, outside the category of presently great powers, would be simply crushed through means of the effects of globalization on such vulnerabilities as their increasing lack of truly sovereign control over the essential portion of the food supplies of their populations as wholes. Therefore those willing nations which represent aggregate great power, must unite to act in defense of the smaller and weaker nations, for the defense and promotion of the common good.

The recently failed Copenhagen Conference on Climate Change, ironically, inaugurated one of the worst winters in a hundred years. Here, a report in the British press.

The broader effect of this intended set of developments, featured the pestilences known as "globalization," and a "unitary Presidency," as part of the wrecking of the U.S. economy itself, especially under the Presidencies of George W. Bush, Jr., and, now, that of a Barack Obama who has already been seen, with good reason, as enjoying the most rapid, and presently accelerating, and richly deserved rate of successful gain of unpopularity of any U.S. President of recent history.

The principal correlative of the British imperial policy and influence to this effect, has been the continuing intention, as I have already noted, as being expressed by the hateful role of the British Consort Prince Philip, to reduce the world's population from a presently estimable level of about 6.7 billions, to less than 2 billions. The recently failed Copenhagen "summit," which, ironically, inaugurated what has been described in such terms as "the worst winter cold wave in an estimated span of a hundred years," featured commitments in the direction of that outcome. Now, despite that failure of the present British monarchy's evil attempt on that occasion, those who are to be regarded by some as the children of Satan, remain disposed to "try again," as early and often, and as widespread as possible.

Those foregoing, selected, crucial facts, respecting the developments of the recent two decades of this planet's history, also have a crucially relevant preceding, 1945-1989 interval of history. That is to speak of the wrong turn made, by what was then the greatest power on this planet at that time, the U.S.A. under U.S. President Harry S Truman.

That was not only a bad turn in U.S. policy; it proved to have been a wrong turn in world history, made under the influence, over Truman, of Britain's Prime Minister Winston Churchill and of economist John Maynard Keynes. It was an onslaught of moral corruption launched, on April 13, 1945, on the occasion of the day after the death of President Franklin D. Roosevelt whose cause President Harry S Truman promptly betrayed.

The Consequences So Far

In effect, the United States under President Harry S Truman, acted in concert with British imperial interests typified by the role of Prime Minister Winston Churchill,

U.S. Vice President Aaron Burr kills former Treasury Secretary Alexander Hamilton, in the infamous duel of July 11, 1804. Traitor Burr, the founder of the Bank of Manhattan, was the personal asset of the British Foreign Office's Jeremy Bentham.

a concert which restored colonialist rule immediately in many parts of the world at that time, and thus unleashed a process of corrosion or outright reversal of the U.S. policy-commitments which had been adopted under President Franklin D. Roosevelt.

This was a corrosion, launched by Britain through setting the nuclear powers of that time against one anothers' throats, a corrosion which has led, over a half-century, with some detours here and there, toward the presently threatened plunge of the entire planet into a chain-reaction like collapse of the planet, a plunge to the present verge of a presently onrushing, planet-wide New Dark Age comparable to, but worse than that of the late Fourteenth Century Europe.

There is no proper mystery concerning the identity of the relevant interests which launched what became that post-April 12, 1945 reversal of U.S. policy under President Harry S Truman.

Over the longer term since the beginning of the so-called "Seven Years War," the power of those British imperialist interests, has tended to increase, despite some most notable intervening periods of set-backs. So matters have stood since the immediate aftermath of

that February 1763 Peace of Paris, a time when the British East India Company, led by figures such as Lord Shelburne, established that Company itself as, essentially, a privately owned empire, and, in 1782, launched the British Foreign Office as its instrument of attempted imperialist mismanagement of the planet as a whole, as it has been from that time, to the present day.

A broad summary of the relevant history since those times, is required at this point, such that the relevant discussion would treat the span of these developments since the British crushing of the rights of the Massachusetts of the Winthrops and Mathers, and since the subsequent death of England's Queen Anne, as a lawful historical process, a process, rather than a mere chronicle of several selected choices from among recent history's events.

It was on or about the exact date of the February 1763 Paris treaty, and the accompanying end of the so-called "French and Indian Wars," that the social forces of the North American English-speaking population of the United States of America were, and remain divided, to the present day, between, on the one side, those in the tradition of predecessors who repelled the tyrannical and predatory measures of the British East India Company, and that opposing part of the population which is customarily identified with "Wall Street" as with the American traitors of Wall Street and kindred pedigrees, traitors such as the British Foreign Office's and Jeremy Bentham's personal asset Aaron Burr, the founder of the Bank of Manhattan.

Since that time, American and British English-speaking wit has referred to the conflicts between the United States and the British empire, still today, as a people divided by the ability to quarrel through the greater efficiency afforded by the use of a common language. So, over the relevant passage of time, since February 1763, within both the United Kingdom and the U.S. Republic, there have been both imperialist and anti-imperialist currents in opposition to one another. The following considerations are indispensable for our purposes here.

Foremost, it must be emphasized that the British empire is not essentially a rule by what British usage identifies as the United Kingdom's "subjects," but, like all European empires which have existed since the aftermath of the Peloponnesian Wars, the British Empire has been, still today, a global, imperial tyranny organized as a system of money, a monetary system, a form of imperial tyranny best recognized when it is seen as expressed in its most naked form as a doctrine of "free trade" which has been imposed upon nations other than Britain, or as the castration of the fatherhoods of continental Europe, as through the subjugation of certain once-proud sovereigns of continental Europe as victims of what is termed "The Euro" and the so-called "Lisbon Treaty."

Traitors, or fools sympathetic to the British empire, as found among the opposition to the U.S.A.'s constitutional system, are the keystone of Britannia's grand scheme for early onset of British imperial, virtually one-world rule over the entire planet, now.

History as a Process

Looking back in time, the distinct form of European imperialism against which we must act today, emerged during the course and aftermath of the Peloponnesian Wars, as a form of rule based on the special quality of a maritime empire which was based on that common principle of monetarism, which has been the actual characteristic of European imperialism, since the Peloponnesian War, up to the present time: after duly noting such exceptions as the reign of Charlemagne, and, later, the temporary role, through the time of the reign of France's Louis XI, of that great principle of the Fifteenth-century Council of Florence put forward by Nicholas of Cusa.

The distilled essence of European imperialism, British imperialism most notably, has been the intent to establish and maintain an enforced, predatory doctrine of "free trade," especially on other peoples' nations, with the imperialists' strong opposition, at most times, to the practice of any form of what is called "protectionism," as such tyranny of "free trade" is to be recognized in the presently, British-led attacks on the stability of the economy of China, from both London and London's fellow-travellers in Washington.

The typical expression of British imperialism today, is the transfer of production of goods from nations with the world's leading technological advantages, to labor-intensive production transferred to cheap-labor markets, as had been done in the British imperialist operations against occupied India in Shelburne's, Bentham's, and Palmerston's time, then, and against China, today.

The typical method of British imperialism, is a practice which echoes the Roman Empire, a practice of organizing warfare and revolutions among targeted nations, as to be recognized in the manner in which the British empire's then-young Foreign Office orchestrated the French Revolution and the Napoleonic wars. These developments are to be recognized, as echoes of the method used to establish the British Empire, as, initially, an empire of the British East India Company, at the 1763 Peace of Paris. We must see this again, in the launching of so-called "World War I" and in London's orchestration of the rise of the Adolf Hitler regime through such channels as the offices of the Bank of England and, also, the formation of the Basel, Switzerland Bank for International Settlements.

It is to be seen again, in the way in which Britain adjusted its course, when it had been confronted with the aftermath of what German forces and the pro-fascist French government of the time had carefully pre-arranged as the Wehrmacht defeat of the physically superior military forces of France, in 1940, which took a much dismayed, formerly Hitler-oriented Britain by surprise.[1] Britain then turned to a United States which it had earlier hoped to ruin.

What I have just written here are, admittedly, harsh truths for many in the world today, but they are the truths which, unless accepted, outline the threat of doom which must be clearly foreseen now, if a global dark age of all humanity is to be avoided during the immediate months ahead.

I. The Productive Powers of Labor

The principal source of the weakness which the nations of Europe, Asia, and the Americas have shown in modern times, until now, has been their susceptibility to the popularized, but mistaken notion, that monetary values are the measure of relative present and future wealth of nations. For precisely such reasons, nearly all notable would-be economic forecasters have failed, repeatedly, during recent decades. For that reason, my own repeated successes as a forecaster have been relatively unique.

To understand how economic processes actually

---

1. It should be evident, that, under Lord Shelburne's leading role in the 1782 establishing of the original British Foreign Office as the key political instrument of the imperialist British East India Company at that time, and that Foreign Office's role in the orchestration of the induced self-inflicted ruin of the French monarchy over the course of the 1782-1789 interval.

Albert Einstein's appreciation of Kepler's discovery produced the famous notion of a finite, but not bounded universe, otherwise known as an anti-entropic, Riemannian universe. Shown: Einstein with his wife, Elsa.

function, we must downgrade the value placed upon the practice of financial forecasting, that we might adopt the advantages of the preferable course provided for the understanding of the real, which is to say physical, economy, as this is preference is facilitated by relying upon Academician V.I. Vernadsky's functional subdivision of known creation among the scientifically principled categories of Lithosphere, Biosphere, and Noösphere.

This is the standpoint of what I have defined as a science of physical economy, in opposition to the intrinsically incompetent notion of a monetarist economy.

As I have done on this account, we must proceed together from the standpoint of the great Bernhard Riemann's discovery of principle, as that discovery, presented in his 1854 habilitation dissertation, provided the essential, revolutionary foundations, made in the footsteps of Gottfried Leibniz, for the principal set of accomplishments of Academician V.I. Vernadsky and Albert Einstein.

Viewing matters in that context, all known forms of existence known to us from consideration of the known universe, up to the present time, express that notion of universal, specifically anti-entropic creativity which the late Albert Einstein identified in his assessment of the great uniquely original discoveries of gravitation by Johannes Kepler, as expressing a universe which is "finite but unbounded" in principle.

This notion is of crucial importance for establishing shared recognition of the principle of progress on which rescue of a presently imperilled planet might be accomplished.

So, following the great principle set forth by Bernhard Riemann, the Lithosphere and Biosphere, are characterized by an inherent, anti-entropic creativity, but only mankind, in our species' character as the expression of the Noösphere, expresses a consciously willful creativity.

So, whereas inanimate and living processes of plant and animal life are distinguished by Einstein's principle of a finite-but-unbounded creativity, only the human individual expresses creativity and its effects as a consciously willful quality of process, as is implicitly typical of the first Chapter of the Christian **Genesis**. This distinction is expressed by the growth of human populations through the benefits of combined scientific and related cultural progress, a willful characteristic of mankind which is not expressed by any other known form of existing living species.

Nations must cease their tendency to maintain the habit of living only in the past. Unlike the beasts, men and women are creative beings from that future which they must bring into existence, as the future colonization of our Moon and of the planet Mars suggests today.

The increase of the human species, is, thus, bounded by mankind's willful ability and disposition to create the improvements of the environment on which the sustaining, and the improvement of the condition of the human population depends. The present urgency of accelerated reliance on the development and proliferation of nuclear-fission and thermonuclear-fusion sources of power, together with the duty of exploring our Solar system—and the universe beyond—exemplifies the present requirement for meeting what are the presently foreseeable of the essential existential needs, and proper aims of all mankind.

Sandia Laboratory's Z-pinch accelerator, part of its fusion research program, releases roughly 80 times the entire world's output of electricity for a few trillionths of a second.

Among such as the empires of the past, the ordinary people have been largely treated as cattle might be treated, as bounded to a fixed order of what is sometimes described as "zero technological growth." The human species, which the great Academician Vernadsky showed to be essentially a creature of the Noösphere, not the Biosphere, expresses its humanity as a servant of the bringing into being of the future, leaving the silly notion of men and women as like the apes, more and more behind.

That distinction of mankind from other forms of life, compels us to take into account the fact that, whereas, mankind, thus far, has relied upon the favorable concentrations of the stock of the preferred elements of the Periodic Table left behind, as in use of the remains of dead plants and animals from the past content of the Lithosphere and Biosphere: The relative depletion of the relatively richest such deposits, requires an increase in the applicable energy-flux-density employed as the means to offset the relative depletion of the richer concentrations of deposits left behind from the past of the Lithosphere and Biosphere.

This requirement is satisfied, most essentially, by the development of the creative powers of the individual human mind experienced in the relevant language-cultures of respectively sovereign nations. Such is the root of the role of sovereign nation-state cultures, a role which separates civilized society from the Biblical horrors of a legendary Tower of Babel. It is the cooperation among such sovereigns, to the effect of fulfilling the just common aims of mankind, as mankind, not as beasts, which is the only tolerable form of composition of the family of nations.

Thus, the common great folly of what is to be called the imperialism of all monetary systems which employ reliance on the use of money as a reigning standard of value, when that notion of relative value is substituted for the appropriate, contrary standard of the increase of the science-driven, Classical-culture-driven productive powers of labor. It is advances in a science- and Classical-culture-driven form of increase of the relative, physical capital-intensity of development of basic economic infrastructure, and in production of means of existence, which provides the only truly scientific measure of economic performance of nations, and of the planet as a whole.

Such is to be taken as the proper meaning of the expression: "the common aims of mankind."

Man must not seek to live as a parasite upon the given state of our planet. We must earn the right to our existence, which must be accomplished through those improvements in the planet on which the proper existence of any sustainable scale of our populations depends. It must be noted that the archeological distinction of man from beasts is man's successful use of the principle of "fire."

The maintenance and improvement of the human condition has required the shift to forms of "fire" of increasing energy-flux density, such that only such means as nuclear fission and, prospectively, thermonuclear fusion, meet mankind's requirements for both the present and the immediately foreseeable generations of mankind. To reject those imperatives is to degrade mankind to the perilous conditions of mere beasts.

Thus, for the foreseeable future of human existence during the remainder of this presently young century, the emphasis is presently on the succession of nuclear fission and thermonuclear fusion, as the precondition for human existence within a range reaching, apparently, today, to the future through which man may reach to a foreseeable future place in the orbit of Mars, a goal which could not be achieved by living human beings without thermonuclear fusion, as by helium-3 isotope as fuel, as the source of the impulse needed.

That perspective is implicitly expressed at this time as the perspective of the leading nations of Asia, and also the Americas, nations whose opportunities for the future are presently bounded, chiefly, implicitly, by leading emphasis upon the regions of the Arctic, and the Pacific and Indian oceans.

To bring about, and maintain such a humanist perspective for all mankind, it is indispensable that our implicit commitment must be to what is regarded as the spiritual aspect of human life which distinguishes man's creativity from the ways of the beast, while taking into account our responsibility for the care of those forms of life expressed by plants and beasts.

Such are the essential expressions of the notion of "the common aims of mankind."

II. Capital Investment Cycles

There are two principal kinds of categorical distinctions for the role of capital-investment cycles in national and world economy. It were convenient to name the available distinctions as being either *physical* or *spiritual*.

Under "physical" we consider two general types: *basic economic physical infrastructure*, and physical capital employed by mankind as *means of production*.

Under "spiritual," we should place *artistic creativity*, including both *great Classical art-forms* and, also, those acts of *scientific discoveries of universal physical principles*.

Viewed from the vantage-point of modern European culture, the meaning of the category of "physical" is relatively more obvious, but it is, as to be indicated here below, only deceptively obvious. The category of "spiritual" is typified by what is entirely lacking in the systemically bestial outlook encountered among the behaviorists of both the current U.S. Obama administration, and British Fabian and like ideologues generally.

The relevant, errant, widespread reductionist presumption of empiricists has been the wrong-headed, if nonetheless widespread notion, that physical science is rooted in mathematics as such, as the errant case of the Euclidean tradition illustrates the folly of attempts to substitute a-prioristic forms of sense-perceptual assumptions respecting sensory effects, for physical principles. Creativity pertains to new discoveries of physical principle, a process of discovery which bounds the domains within which a competent mathematics may roam, but only under appropriate physical conditions, as Bernhard Riemann emphasized, with delicious irony, in the concluding single sentence of his Earth-shaking 1854 habilitation dissertation.

So, discovery of physically efficient principles occurs as Albert Einstein identified this, in the instances of Johannes Kepler's uniquely original discovery of the principle of the planetary orbit, and the subsequent, uniquely original discovery of the general principle of gravitation (contrary to the Isaac Newton hoax), as in Kepler's **The Harmony of the Worlds**, or in the discovery of the principle of least action by Pierre de Fermat, or the great discovery of Bernhard Riemann in his 1854 habilitation dissertation, or the fundamental Seventeenth and early Eighteenth centuries' contributions of Gottfried Leibniz.

A comparable case of the principle of human creativity, is the development of the concept of well-tempered counterpoint by Johann Sebastian Bach. The concluding paragraph of Percy Bysshe Shelley's **A Defence of Poetry**, is a highly relevant sort of comparable case, as it is also an extension of Gottfried Leibniz's discovery of the principle of physical dynamics into the rightful domain of Classical artistic composition.

In brief, man is not the subject of mathematics; rather, competent application of mathematics is a subject of that principle of the human creativity which governs physical scientific progress, but whose natural habitat is Classical musical counterpoint and poetry, the domain of the ironically creative powers of a Leibniz, a Riemann, a Vernadsky, and an Einstein, powers which distinguish the human mind from the domain of the beasts.

The connection of what is identified as the relationship of the spiritual power of Classical expressions of individual human creativity, to successes in progress in economic processes, points to a factor of practically adducible, personal immortality in the legacies of great scientific minds and Classical poets alike.

That is to emphasize that whereas there is no evidence of physical immortality of a living human being as such, the creative works of great individual minds typify the meaning of human individual immortality, the powerful, implicitly immortal imprint of discoveries of principle, as in Classical science and poetry. Since those discoveries of principles live on as still efficiently acting within the culture long after the author is deceased, their approximate immortality of those discoveries as efficiently acting ideas, is often an efficient cause within the development of society, long into the future, even permanently part of mankind in what is sometimes identified as "a simultaneity of eternity."

So, we may say that the virtue of immortality lies in the efficient expression of a discovery of a principled conception, such as an efficiently acting principle of physical science, a principle which remains efficiently active, and is still changing the state of the world, long after the author is deceased, as, for example, for the ancient Archytas and Plato, or the Classical Aeschylus.

Thus, the essential form of human morality within history, is expressed by the individual's devotion to the accomplishment of discovery and development of ideas whose effect reaches, efficiently, far beyond the boundaries of the discoverer's mortal existence. Thus, truly creative human individuals who have died, live on ef-

Academician V.I. Vernadsky with his daughter, Nina, during the 1910s. Discoveries of principles live on long after the author is deceased, in what is sometimes identified as "a simultaneity of eternity."

ficiently in the future progress of society, in the future of humanity, as through both discoverers of scientific principle, or, in the fashion of John Keats' **Ode on a Grecian Urn**.

The essential, shall we say "constitutional" principle of a good society, is the devotion to the improvement of the future of mankind. This point is expressed by such forms as, "What can you expect to achieve as a contribution to mankind, between now and the time of your passing from life in society?" "What can you, while still living, give as a still efficient form of action, to the future of mankind?" It is only people so inspired, who love future mankind so much, that they can be really trusted with spiritual guidance of the role assigned to government for the future of mankind.

The Human Mind

Today, not only do the benefits of modern society's cultural development permit an increase of the number of years a typical individual may reach, not only is the functional power of the individual increased and made more enduring; it is shown that the powers of the mind may be even increased in certain crucial respects, as reflections which amount to an improvement in society's knowledge of principle, as by those considered very old.

The view, such as that of the British behaviorists in the tradition of Adam Smith's **Theory of the Moral Sentiments**, degrades human beings to the same status as those beasts who are slaughtered when their continued existence is deemed to be inconvenient, as for the war-time Nazi regime in Germany, or the authors of the death-care policies of Britain's Prime Minister Tony Blair, or in the worse than prospective, Hitlerian, current health-care doctrines of a U.S. Obama administration.

For such people as those latter, especially those with official authority in society, the rights of the human individual can not be distinguished systemically from that of farm animals or wild game, as Smith makes that implied point systemically, in that location, and as the neo-malthusian policies of the present British Royal House and of the U.S. Obama administration represent an inhuman spirit of evil today.

The behaviorists, like the President Obama who echoes the image of the personal character of the mass-murderous reign of the Roman Emperor Nero, reject provable principles of specifically human practice by mere statistical inferences, thus bringing a society fallen into the likeness of their prey, into precisely the kind of bestiality for which the war-time Hitler regime became notorious, but, this time, with Britain's Prince Philip and Tony Blair, or President Obama, they spread a degree of evil on an intended, global scale far beyond that of the Hitler regime at the worst of its actual practice.

With persons sharing such bestialized views as those associated with that part of the Obama administration or the British monarchy presently in power, the fate of mankind as a whole must be considered as in immediate jeopardy. Without the mustering of a superior power from among nations, the planet as a whole could not be secured against the relative immediacy of the most monstrous action against humanity which has been known to mankind thus far.

Whereas, the recurrence of such global threats, presently, which echo the precedent of the war-time Hitler regime, requires preventive actions now, the recurrence of such threats could not be prevented without the institutionalization of a self-conception, by mankind, of the beauty of mankind's efficiently conceived options for society's better future.

Morality is to be found by each generation in its mission-oriented devotion to some form of betterment for mankind within the full span of a generation's future life-time, and beyond that. Without that, morality is merely a convention without efficient substance, and therefore as easily cast aside as by Hitler earlier, or the British monarchy and its U.S. fellow-travelers such as those of the behaviorists of the Obama administration of today.

III. The Space in Which To Live

Now, let us consider a crucially important principle of future government on this planet: the nature of actual human creativity.

The presently immediate boundaries of mankind's future habitation during the remainder of this yet young century, are identified as comprising the space marked out presently by the planet Earth, Earth's Moon, and Mars. When we consider this development as a process of enlarging mankind's habitat, as we must do so presently, the language of "physical space-time" takes on a different meaning than has been customary, even among many relevant scientists up to this time. It refers, now, to living and breeding in broader realms than merely within the range of physical-space-time of this marked-out region within the Solar system.

In relevant discussions of policy as developed since the Germany space-pioneers of the 1920s, and, again, as in the Soviet Union, western Europe, and the U.S.A. during the post-1945 decades, the emphasis has lain on the use of development of industries on Earth's Moon for creating the means for human travel between Earth's orbiting Moon and an orbiting base above Mars.

During the post-World War II years, Wernher von Braun evoked the image of Christopher Columbus' use of a flotilla of craft for reaching Mars from Earth. Since that time, additional difficulties have become clear. Essentially three hundred days, or more, of transit from our orbiting Moon to the lunar orbit of Mars, have forced serious attention to the problems of lack of a suitable gravitational field for the security of the interplanetary travelers, in addition to the problems posed for human beings on our Moon, and, also, on the surface of Mars.

If we examine the history of physical science since the work of such followers of Carl F. Gauss and Bernhard Riemann, in their time, and consider the progress

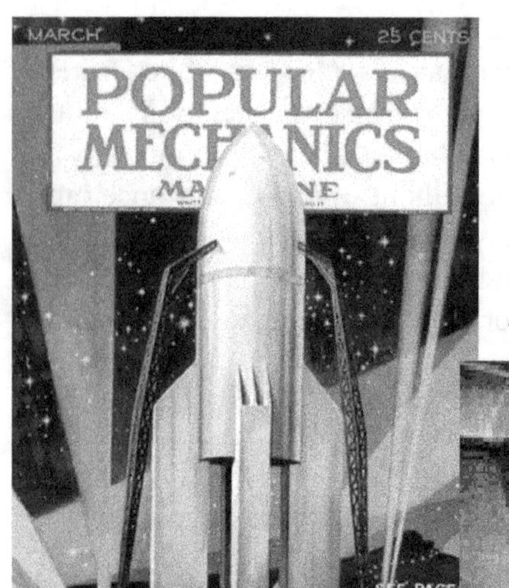

German space pioneer Hermann Oberth was the technical advisor for Fritz Lang's 1929 film "Frau im Monde" ("Woman on the Moon"). With the movie's poster on its cover, the American magazine Popular Mechanics *illustrates how this highly accurate portrayal of space flight inspired people worldwide. Inset: a scene from the film.*

in related matters of science up through the success of the U.S.A. organization of a Moon landing, we are encouraged to use the pre-1815 Ecole Polytechnique of such as Gaspard Monge, Lazare Carnot, and Alexander von Humboldt and his famous protégé Lejeune Dirichlet, as mapping-points for assessment of the rates of fundamental progress, or, in the alternative, also certain disgusting incompetencies introduced into physical science since the early years of the Nineteenth Century. We think of the birth of an interval of three coming generations, born during this century, since the present time, of which two will have had a considerable possibility to have come, freshly, to an age-level of scientific or Classical artistic maturity.

In adopting such a working perspective, we are confronted, at least implicitly so, with the following, relevant, great moral issue.

The behaviorists, including the existentialists, who have tended to dominate the policy-shaping of the nations of Europe and the Americas, more and more, during the successive post-1945 generations of trans-Atlantic cultures, have been an intrinsically immoral body in their influence on society and history generally.

It has been the systematic destruction of those creative powers of the human mind which are associated with both Classical artistic composition and physical-scientific creativity, which has been the leading correlative of both the artistic and scientific-economic decadence of society since the death of U.S. President Franklin Roosevelt, a decadence most clearly identified with the influence of the kind of depravity associated with that justly infamous Bertrand Russell who proposed a preventive nuclear attack upon the Soviet Union, an attack intended to bring about that imposition of world government, which remains the intent of the current British monarchy today.

On this account, the following exposition is required. I proceed, thus, as follows.

The Subject of Human Nature

Physically, the preconditions for the continued existence of civilized society, require a rate of progress expressed as advances in the productive powers of labor, per capita and per square kilometer, advances which offset, and must overcome the lawful tendency for depletion of the richest concentrations of those resources on which the maintenance of an existing quantity and quality of human life in society depends. *The law is: progress, or begin to die.*

That indispensable progress is expressed, not exclusively, but typically, in both advances in what is Classical artistic and language culture, and in the increase of the net productive powers of labor through effects of physical-scientific advances.

That notion of the necessity of human progress, confronts mankind with the necessity of progress as the highway to the future existence of a society's culture. We must, therefore, learn from past experience, but must not limit ourselves to lessons from past experience. *Civilized mankind is a maker of a future which had not been achieved through earlier habits.*

So, Albert Einstein, writing on the subject of the uniquely original discovery of a principle of universal gravitation by Johannes Kepler, thus defined the universe expressed by Kepler's uniquely original discovery, as *finite, but not bounded.* It is a universe which does not exist in mere time; but, rather, time exists only within physical space-time. The Riemannian metric of physical space-time, is the transformation of human existence to a higher order of being, through the realization of the equivalent of valid discoveries of universal

EIRNS/Philip Ulanowsky

Dr. Robert Moon, the renowned physicist who worked on the Manhattan Project, teaches youngsters at a summer program in Northern Virginia in 1983. "Morality," writes LaRouche, "is a dedication to the changes which are the necessary advances to a required change of state which we must bring about in the future we bequeath to our progeny."

physical space-time.

Thus, society exists within the bounds of the realization of those discoveries which create a state of existence which had not existed earlier: thus, expressing a principle of universal anti-entropy. Wisdom lies not in the experience of the past, but in the creation of the future, better condition which had not existed in the past. *Finite, but not bounded.*

This view of the matter is the basis for true morality. We must learn what happened in the past; but, that is not the source of the future. Take the following illustration of what I have just outlined in the immediately preceding paragraphs.

Is truth the knowledge of experience one has learned from the past? Or, is truth nothing different than choosing the changes in practice which are the experience of the necessarily chosen new principles which are the means for meeting the new challenge which must be our response to the demands of the oncoming future? *Truth is the passage from the uncompleted past, the finite, into the yet to be experienced future, that which is not bounded.*

What, child, are you going to accomplish which supplies those qualitative changes in practice which the success of the future demands? We must learn from the past, that which the past, *the finite*, has to offer; but,

the knowledge of the past is soon worthless, until we have committed ourselves to something new, *to the unbounded*, the revolution in ideas of practice, which is our necessary choice of access to the necessary future. In this respect, nothing which is truthful, is true, but necessary change to new ways in the future now before us.

For the purpose of practice of society now, we must measure our obligatory performance in terms of a span of two or more generations required as the change of society from a present state of development, to a necessarily future state of development.

In the present, still young century, the indicator of that necessary and possible progress, which we must adopt as our intended future development, touches the matter of facilitating successful human travel, from Earth-orbit, to Mars-orbit, and safe return, an objective which could be attained within reliance upon thermonuclear fusion modalities. *One must live, now, to create the future. That, and nothing different, is morality: the principle of the unbounded.*

That, as I have just described it, is necessarily a true goal for mankind within the range of the new century we have recently entered. However, while that goal is a true one, its most important aspect is that it, as I have said, defines a specific, convenient example of a universal moral principle for society. Morality is not the lesson of past experience; morality is a dedication to the changes which are the necessary advances to a required change of state which we must bring about in the future we bequeath to our progeny.

One child asks another: *"What are you going to have become, when you have grown up?"*

In other words: we live in an anti-entropic universal process of anti-entropic change of universal principle. *That is the essence of human morality.* We are moral only if we do what our grandparents, and parents, did not achieve in the matter of increasing the power of mankind in the universe, qualitatively, per capita and per unit of physical-space-time measure.

It is useful to look at the past history of European

civilization's progress in physical science from the time of Jeanne d'Arc, and, a bit later, Filippo Brunelleschi and Nicholas of Cusa, or from Kepler, Fermat, and Leibniz, and from the Ecole Polytechnique near the beginning of the Nineteenth Century, or from Bernhard Riemann's 1854 habilitation dissertation forward. What must be the chosen destiny of each of the two generations yet to come to full maturity from their birth in the decades of that portion of the remainder of the present century which we entered in the immediately preceding decade? *We are, therefore, morally, what we have chosen to be the better future in which our descendants shall dwell.*

Russia's Trans-Siberian Railway crosses the Kama River, near Perm, in the Urals region.

Such are the terms within which we must define the foreseeable goals of the remainder of this present, still young century before us. That is the relevant definition of political morality among sovereign nations and their peoples today. We must be creators in the image of the Creator. That is a true political morality within and among nations now.

Such are the needed common aims of all mankind. That is the only true morality. That is the only truth.

IV. The Coming of the Railroads

To move forward into the time of the future, society must move forward in space.

Today, the young citizens of the United States are often more ignorant of essentials than their grandparents' generation. How is that proven? Simply ask: what happened to the railroads?

The functional concept of the railroad-system, as a system, was clearly established in intention by the work done by then U.S. Secretary of State John Quincy Adams' defining the policy of establishing the United States as a transcontinental nation, from the Canadian northern border to the Mexican border, at the south, and overland from the Atlantic coast to the Pacific.

To understand this in the way this must become understood in the world today, look always at the future in terms of the change which breaks out of those limits which had reigned in the past.

So, earlier, what became Mediterranean culture, as distinct from the imperial systems of West Asia, was a maritime culture. Roads were a useful but marginal supplement to maritime development. Later, Charlemagne advanced civilization by developing a system of inland waterways, from the Pyrenees northerly and eastward. Later, came the shift from the bounds of the Mediterranean and Black Sea into the Atlantic, with the decline of Byzantium and the Norman Conquest. Then, in the later years of Nicholas of Cusa, came Cusa's imperative for reaching from the Mediterranean across the oceans to the continents on the opposite coasts, the imperative which led to the European settlements in the Americas.

Later, came the trans-continental railway system of the United States, and the resulting shift from within the bounds of the Atlantic and Indian Ocean, through reaching the Pacific coasts of Asia, from the place where the westward coast of the Trans-American railways met the Pacific coast. Then, came the advent of the unification of the railway with those related transcontinental systems uniting Eurasia, the Americas, and Africa into a unified global system. Next, will come the links to the Moon and then Mars.

All of this is unified and subsumed by the increase of the energy-flux density of the leading sources of power which are employed according to that great principle which distinguishes man from the beasts. That principle is the use of forms of fire-power, from simple burning of fuels, to the higher reaches of energy-flux-density associated with nuclear-fission, and then thermonuclear fusion and beyond, as the increasingly mighty source of power on which progress depends.

In that process of transformation of our planet, and into pathways beyond, the power of mankind is increased as a benefit, in physical cost per unit of human action per capita and per square kilometer of territory, as this is fairly measured in terms of what it is convenient to identify as "energy-flux density."

So, the highway from the Earth to the Moon, was built with aid of the technologies of an age of nuclear fission, and so shall we come to establish the virtual pavement through Solar space, from Moon to Mars, the latter a goal which defines the future state of this presently still-young century, through that highway through space defined by thermonuclear fusion, and then beyond.

Why the Railways Were Ruined

The existence of reliable highway systems, was not a mistake; but, tearing down transcontinental railway systems out of preference for highway travel and relatively shorter-term, costly air-transport systems, was a great, and fully intentional setback for mankind.

In the meantime, the most important weakness in railway systems was the failure to develop advances in high-speed transport, failures which are being remedied in some still limited degree by present generations now of high-speed rail and, more significantly, magnetic-levitation systems.

The shift away from railway systems came about through the effects of the British empire's commitment to an attempted destruction of the United States, a commitment which had emerged from the defeat of London's efforts to destroy the United States, through the efforts of the British Empire's Lord Palmerston, in the attempted ruin of China and the use of such British For-

eign Office devices as the revolt of London's treasonously inclined puppet, the Confederacy. This British reaction was expressed, most notably, in the hysterical reaction of the British monarchy to the development of intercontinental Eurasian railway systems which were developed according to the precedent of the model of the U.S. transcontinental railway system, as this was led in Eurasia by the work of Russia's D.I. Mendeleyev and by Germany's Chancellor Bismarck.

So, we must recall an evil British empire's success in bringing about the ouster of Bismarck as part of the British empire's preparation for what were to become known as Britain's launching of what were to be become World Wars I and II. This included, prominently, Prince Albert Edward's enlisting Japan into attacks on China and Russia which were continued from 1895 through 1945, by such continuing means as Britain's enlisting Japan, during the early 1920s, for a plan for a joint British attack on the naval forces and bases of the United States, and by putting the Bank of England's choice, Adolf Hitler, into power in Germany, as also the crucial part which had been played during King Edward VII's heyday, by the assassinations of France's President Sadi Carnot, and U.S. President William McKinley.

So, that tradition which was continued by the British asset and U.S. President Harry S Truman, typified the changes in U.S. policy which had been associated earlier with the same Wall Street extension of the British empire which had backed Adolf Hitler's rise to power in Germany, and which launched the great conflict called World War II.

The post-1945 threat of nuclear warfare, that of 1945-1989, initially on Winston Churchill's behalf, dominated the world's affairs, from the time of Bertrand Russell's 1946, public launching of the policy of an intended, "preventive" nuclear attack on the Soviet Union, on the mistaken presumption that the Soviet Union would not be capable of timely development of nuclear weapons by itself. This direction in trans-Atlantic schemes has been associated, to the present day, with the combination of Britain and Wall Street finance, as continued through the destruction of the sovereignty of the nation-states of continental Europe through the post-1989 initiatives of Britain's asset and Charles de Gaulle-hating French President François Mitterrand, Margaret Thatcher, and the son of Averell Harriman's Prescott Bush.

These observations on the most relevant of the

nearly past two centuries' history of development and ruin of continental mass-transportation systems, are indispensable here, to warn against the short-term thinking, and consequent follies of the strategic thinking of most governments over the course of the time from London's sponsorship, as in Bentham successor Palmerston's time, and later, of the attempted destruction of the economic systems of continental Europe and beyond.

To understand the grand scale on which history actually unfolds, we must free leaders of nations from the typically deluded, relatively short-term, "who hit whom" mentality which had led what should have been great nations and cultures to engage in the follies through which sovereign nations destroy themselves in prolonged military and related conflicts modeled on Britain's orchestration of the ruin of continental Europe through repeated copying of the chronic stupidity known as the recurrence of the mutual ruin of continental Europe through the long wars in, chiefly, Eurasia. These are the wars on which the rise of the British empire has based its power in the world, to the present day, as we have just recently experienced this again, in Her Britannic Majesty's attempted imperial destruction of civilization itself, through the so-called Copenhagen conference.

Such are the precedents for the abominable role of a pro-treasonous, pro-genocidal policy-making under a follower of Britain's, lying, evil follower of the World War II health-care followers of Adolf Hitler, such as former Prime Minister Tony Blair, and Blair's follower in such pro-genocidal policies as President Barack Obama up to the present time.

We must, in particular, reach the happier state of mind, in which we act on the premise of understanding the essential difference between the necessity of respectively sovereign nation-states and the common, global interest which should, at the same time, unite the sovereign nations of the planet around policy-objectives worthy of the title, "the common aims of mankind."

The great transportation and other physical systems, and the sharing of advances in science and technology, typify the means by which the aims of the nations of mankind are united, at the same moment that their cooperation is rooted in the principle of separation by reliance of each upon the indispensable instrument of national cultural sovereignty.

Thus far in history, the attempt to effect a system of nation-states which, while perfectly sovereign, are united by a common, subsuming objective for all nations, has been a net failure. We should recognize this from the examples of the war which Britain waged against the people of North America even before the 1776-1782 warfare for freedom, and in the subsequent schemes of Palmerston against the U.S. republic. Such were the British imperial impulses which caused two so-called "world wars" which were each organized by the initiatives of the British empire, and by the prolonged, so-called "Cold War," and by Britain's ruin of the sovereign nations of continental Europe since 1989, to the present date, as by Queen Elizabeth II's continuing attempts at destruction of the United States of America at the present instant.

All nations do have an adducible common interest in the general welfare of humanity, if we have the wisdom to recognize that fact. That common interest is expressed by the role of national sovereignty in bringing each people up to their highest potential for self-development of a national culture, and of the cooperation to that end shared among those national cultures. Regrettably, the effort has been limited, more often, to minimize the intensity of conflict, rather than growing together, separately, but fraternally, through the development of our understanding of the common cause which unites us in great enterprises such as the present prospect for the development of nearby space.

As the great Aeschylus has warned us, still today, as in his **Prometheus Trilogy**, it is the fight against prohibition of the use of "fire," such as the fiery power of nuclear fission, which distinguishes the morality of the human species from the bestiality of systems of slavery and serfdom, and which pits humanity against forms of society which impose upon societies that tendency for backwardness and irrationalism which has been the most significant common factor in man's oppression of fellow-man, and in rendering men and women stupefied through aid of such wicked opposition to the advancement, as through forms of fire, of each and all people's power to exist.

Today, the lever by which we may be able to effect a unification of respective sovereigns in common concern, and common means, is the evolution of the modes of power and transportation needed to unite mankind's nations on this planet to common ends, and in common efforts in space beyond.

President Theodore Roosevelt shovels dirt from the Panama Canal onto Colombia, in this cartoon by W.A. Rogers from the New York Herald, *December 1903. Teddy Roosevelt—quite different from his cousin Franklin— was a British stooge and pro-malthusian.*

What Went Wrong in America?

Leading circles from among nations around the world, should consider a curious fact.

That fact is, that under the influence of a President Theodore Roosevelt, a cousin in flesh, but not spirit, of the later President Franklin D. Roosevelt, a pro-malthusian policy was advanced, as through the role of Theodore Roosevelt in the United States. This was done to the intended effect, that virtually no significant progress was allowed in the development of the land-area of a vast region from a point to the west of the Mississippi River and the western mountain ranges of California. This was the effect of Theodore Roosevelt's adaptation of the Malthusian dogma to the Wall Street-centered, policy-shaping repertoires in the United States. This fact should not be received as surprising news, since, after all, Theodore Roosevelt's uncle, who trained him, had been the London-based chief of the Confederacy's intelligence services during the course of the famous U.S. Civil War which Britain had orchestrated against the existence of the United States.

This same, recurring pattern of British imperialism, still today, is also highly relevant, both as a crucial fact of modern history since the 1756-1763 "Seven Years War" in Europe, and as expressive of the way which what became known as World War I was brought into being.

Prior to the related facts of the ouster of Germany's Chancellor Bismarck, who was an intellectual ally of the United States, and of the assassination of France's President Sadi Carnot, Bismarck and the United States had been of a converging opinion respecting the wickedness of the Prince of Wales later known as Edward VII. Moreover, the great German economic reforms under Bismarck, had been premised on the successes of the United States' policies, and the leading circles of the U.S.A. such as Henry C. Carey. Carey and Germany's Bismarck circles shared much sense of a common mission for mankind, which both had shared in common with the leading circles of Russia at that time.

In fact, Bismarck, for as long as he remained Chancellor, was the block which prevented the Prince of Wales from launching a war between Germany and Russia, a war organized by Britain through the manipulation of a stupid Habsburg Kaiser intent on fomenting a religious war in the Balkans, a war whose principal intent, was the intent of Britain's Prince Albert Edward to pit Russia and Germany against one another, that for the purpose, as Bismarck himself described British intent, to ruin the continent of Europe once more, with a new version of the 1756-1763 "Seven Years War."

As long as Bismarck remained Chancellor of Germany, and as long as President William McKinley remained U.S. President, Prince Albert Edward's intention to ruin continental Europe with a "world war," was blocked.

There were chiefly three factors employed in Prince Albert Edward's pre-launching of what was to become known as 'World War I." First, the assassination of France's President Sadi Carnot. Second, Prince Albert Edward's seducing Japan into commitment to a war against both China and Russia which would continue from 1895 to August 1945, and the later, 1920s commitment of Japan to an attack on the U.S. naval base at Pearl Harbor which was planned by agreement between London and Japan. Third, that assassination of U.S. President William McKinley, which brought the nephew of a British-owned U.S. traitor, Theodore Roosevelt, into the Presidency, thus switching the U.S.A.

King Edward VII (Prince Albert Edward before his coronation) successfully brought about the ouster of German Chancellor Otto von Bismarck (right) in 1890. This wrecked the drive for American-style economic policies, while paving the way for World War I.

away from friendship with Bismarck's Germany, as under McKinley, to the side of the British Empire.

The special case of Japan's remaining an ally of Britain against both China and Russia, must be summarily clarified at this point.

That case must be considered in light of the fact that Britain had been allied with Japan against Russia, since approximately 1895, until the British fleet was put at risk of being taken over by Hitler. The defeat of France impelled Winston Churchill to play his part in the role of switching to the side of the U.S.A. out of fear that control over Europe by Hitler would lead quickly to the destruction of the British empire itself. That was an empire which Britain could not continue to defend by an alliance with France, once France itself had been conquered by Germany.

Japan could not make a comparable switch away from an alliance, especially since Japan's new situation had already led it into combining a "Go South" element with its existing commitments to destruction of the U.S.A. as well as China and Russia. Japan stayed, uncomfortably, with Hitler, all of which, on Japan's part, was a legacy of what had been, until the fall of France, the British alliance with Japan, against Britain's former Pearl Harbor target of the 1920s, the U.S.A., in addition

to the original Japan alliance against China and Russia.

In all of this, of course, Wall Street was always both, chiefly, an asset, but also an ally of the British empire, as Wall Street is a British asset, rather than a loyal representative of the U.S.A., as has been the case since the February 1763 Peace of Paris, as the case of the 1925 court-martial of U.S. General Mitchell also shows. That is key to the implicitly treasonous, presently continuing "bail-out" policy of U.S. Representative Barney Frank, and also of U.S. President Barack Obama throughout the 2007-2010 interval to the present date.

Such was also my own personal experience, in Burma (Myanmar) and India during 1945-1946, which virtually all alert U.S. military personnel in the region experienced on the ground during that same period of time.

The U.S. Railroads

The U.S. railway system had continued to play a leading, if waning role in U.S. economic development until about 1924-1926, but was revived from threatened ruin by the Presidency of Franklin Roosevelt. The U.S. railway system played a leading logistical role in the mobilization for the U.S.A. role in World War II, and in the development of the U.S. economy, and the war-mobilization, under President Franklin Roosevelt.

However, the ongoing development of the U.S. national-defense highway system took hold during the middle through late 1950s, as signalled by the Wall Street-steered, ill-fated outcome of the negotiations between the Pennsylvania and New York Central railway systems, and the automobile was used as the bait to induce the U.S. population to participate in a long-term process of the destruction of its own national economy.

The last gasp of an attempt to return the U.S. economy to sane policy overall, collapsed with the assassination of President John F. Kennedy.

The relevant trend toward recurring new wars in the image of the Seven Years War, as during what has been now more than a century of a trend in world history had actually begun with that 1890 ouster of Chancellor Bis-

Library of Congress

U.S. railroad workers in 1942. The system played a key role in the mobilization for World War II, under President Franklin D. Roosevelt.

marck, which opened the doors for what was to become World War I. Prior to the 1890s generally, and the assassination of U.S. President McKinley in particular, there had been a deep friendship among the United States, Germany, and Russia, in opposition to British imperialism, a tradition traced back to Catherine the Great's role in leading that League of Armed Neutrality which made the establishment of the United States possible, a friendship with Russia which had also played a crucial role in assisting U.S. defense against the British Empire's controlling hand in deploying the Confederacy as a puppet of London.

Indeed, truth be told, it was the British Empire itself which was actually responsible for the organizing of what became World Wars I and II, and much other evil, betwixt and between. It was a treasonous impulse within the United States, an impulse rooted in the British East India Company's control of what became traitor Aaron Burr's Wall Street, since the February 1763 Peace of Paris, which has been the crucial factor in all of the great folly and wickedness displayed by leading political forces, the so-called "Wall Street gang," since that time.

It is the same thing to be witnessed in the roles of President George W. Bush, Jr., and President Barack Obama's (and Representative Barney Frank's) incumbency thus far. All known history is not a series of dis-

crete events, but, rather, an evolving, dynamic process, reaching far back to times before an actual history of mankind has been known.

Therefore, the only competent remedies for the evils which mankind in general has suffered to our present knowledge of history thus far, are those actions which have been shaped intentionally by insight into the means for gaining willful control over the continuing process of history since ancient times unknown, to the present day, rather than debating the issue of which badger slaughtered the creatures in the henhouse last night.

It is breaking the traditional habit of warfare in history, and also in pre-history, which must be the choice of means for escaping the looming onrush of the new, global dark age of all humanity which the currently dominant trends in world affairs threaten to bring upon the entire planet such a very short time, now, ahead. Tradition now threatens the doom of all nations and peoples; if that tradition can not be willfully broken now, by the exceptional means which I present here now, it must then be said that a prolonged great new dark age already grips the entirety of our planet now. Time for changing that trend is now being rapidly exhausted.

That needed change can be made successfully now, if the appropriate forces can be assembled to that end, now.

Unless the common action of an initiating four great powers, as by one, can be launched now by the concerted leading action of the U.S.A., Russia, China, and India, there is no hope in sight for avoiding a prolonged and vast planetary new dark age, now.

The key to the measures which are required for such a noble outcome, are centered on a new form of organization among the sovereign nations of the planet through three leading perspectives. The unification of a planetary system of sovereign nation-states around the common aims of a planetary mass-transit system, a drive to the generalization of the power of nuclear fission and thermonuclear fusion, and the preparations for bringing the organization of the nearby Solar space of Johannes Kepler's Earth, Moon, and Mars, and the Riemannian foundations of the fruitful genius of Academician V.I. Vernadsky and Albert Einstein into play as the leading ideas shaping the presently continuing history of that set of planets, now. Break the mold of slavery to ancient habits, to liberate that great power which is presently locked captive, within.

How National Territory Is Organized

Let us, for the sake of this moment's discussion, treat all forms of ground-based mass transit as a single topic. Now, consider the way in which modes of transportation of both passengers and freight affect the quality of the organization of nationwide and wider territories.

From this standpoint, the post-World War II organization of U.S. territory according to the implications of economy of movement and of production, has been a physical-economic disaster, that on several premises.

The optimal organization of the distribution and local efficiency of the sundry principal qualities of communities, such as urban-residential, urban-commercial, urban-industrial, rural-industrial, rural-agricultural, rural-forestation, major watershed, and reserve territories, have become an economic catastrophe.

For example, density of frequent commuter movements, per capita, should be within a quarter to a half-hour each way, with aid of low-cost-to-passenger, dense, modern commuter systems to produce such an effect.[2] In the greater surrounding region Washington, D.C. region, extending to West Virginia, of high-density commuter activity, for example, commuting time daily ranges up to four hours per day, with soaring fees, large fuel expenses, and an incurred lapsed time which destroys family life.

During the post-1945 interval, especially since the mid-1950s, there has been an accelerating concentration of employment in excessively overgrown urban and suburban regions, while vast expanses of formerly populated regions of agriculture and industry have been abandoned.

In part, these deleterious effects have been by-products of increasing the dependency of commuter life, and related transportation, upon the personal automobile, and even the willful destruction of highly efficient previously existing mass-transport systems. What is also notable about this trend has been the great increase in net cost to society incurred by these shifts.

At the same time, the reliance on the individual automobile for commuting within burgeoning urban and suburban localities, has greatly increased both the paid-out and indirect costs of transportation, relative to the lower costs of modern commuter systems: The increase of direct costs, relative to municipalities of reasonably-sized organization, around low-incurred-cost mass-transit systems, plus the heavy burden of lost "family time" also incurred in this way.

Another, increasingly significant factor, during recent decades since the 1950s in the U.S.A., for example, has been the effect of loss of reliable railway systems for passenger traffic on the characteristics of the air-transport systems. The costs, and lost-time factor in medium-distance passenger air transport, must be compared with high-speed mass rail and comparable ground-transport, as serving as links among urban centers. Overall, the failure to utilize the total territory of the United States efficiently, has had ruinous combined effects, in terms of costs incurred by a wrong choice of modalities in transportation-related factors of both urban and rural life.

High-speed ground-based transport, as by rail or magnetic-levitation systems, is both the optimal policy, and the modality which is optimal for both the people and the productive economy. The over-emphasis on dependency on the private automobile, instead of rail and comparable modes, has been insane, as very costly, in its sundry varieties of effects.

V. The Souls of the People

Mesopotamia has given the world what I regard here as examples of the great disasters which the tendency toward oligarchical cultures has brought, repeatedly, upon mankind. I refer, in the first instance, to the induced decadence which led to the fall of Sumer, and the ruin of the once great Baghdad Caliphate, and, in between, the consequence of the combined effects of the Peloponnesian War and the replacement of the progressive culture typified by Archytas and Plato, as dis-

---

2. For example, until the change which occurred beginning the 1970s, studies showed that the cost of mass-transit within the metropolitan New York City region was less if no fares were collected. Free public rapid-transit was, in physical principle, less costly to the combined passengers and public providers of the municipality providing this service, than a fare-based system. Turnstile society is, inherently, generally, a poorer performer for the economy as a whole, than a free-per-event mode.

tinguished from the accelerated decadence of a drift into an oligarchical decadence which had been associated with Aristotle and his followers.

I also refer to the so-called "oligarchical model" associated with the negotiations between King Philip of Macedon and the Achaemenids.

View those several examples from ancient and medieval history from the standpoint of a similar kind of cultural degeneration which has struck the U.S.A. and Europe from the hands of Truman and Churchill, and in other places, despite what had once been the defeat of the evil Hitler regime in Europe.

I refer to presently continuing, morbid, moral and intellectual disasters, such as the recent pestilences known, variously, as the European Congress for Cultural Freedom (CCF), and the related case of the existentialist movement associated with those so-called "Frankfurt School" existentialists associated with the sometime lovers, Hannah Arendt and the sometime Nazi Martin Heidegger. The point concerning those matters which is of special relevance for this report, is the fact that such intellectual viruses as those have a strong tendency for destruction of the creative potential of the persons drawn into submission to such traditions.

The term "Classical art-forms," when employed in a meaningful way, makes reference to the fact that it is chiefly in Classical artistic compositions, as in the tradition of the Classical school of Eighteenth-century Europe of Johann Sebastian Bach, Wolfgang Mozart, Ludwig Beethoven, and that of Abraham Kästner and such of his associates as Gotthold Lessing and Moses Mendelssohn, and of their follower Friedrich Schiller, or the Classical school in physical science of such followers of Filippo Brunelleschi, Nicholas of Cusa, and such explicit followers of Cusa in science as Leonardo da Vinci, Johannes Kepler, Pierre de Fermat, Gottfried Leibniz, Carl F. Gauss, Lejeune Dirichlet, Bernhard Riemann, and such followers of Riemann as Academician V.I. Vernadsky, and Albert Einstein.

The Classical school is otherwise fairly identified as the disciplined expression of the creative powers of the imagination, as in Johannes Kepler's uniquely original discovery of gravitation, the powers on which all valid discoveries in matters of physical science, and art, depend.

With the post-World War I rise in the influence of the depraved, post-positivist, radical reductionist Ber-

trand Russell and such among Russell's more notorious devotees, such as an angered David Hilbert's rejects, Professor Norbert Wiener and John von Neumann, the creative aspect of science was diminished as the representatives of the older generation, born before, or slightly after so-called World War I, died out, or were simply, frequently passed over, as was even Albert Einstein to a large degree, since the heyday of the Fifth Solvay Conference of 1927, onwards.[3]

The existentialist depravity is fairly treated as an echo of the factor of corruption which struck down Classical Greece's role as a political power during the Peloponnesian War. The rise of Aristotle's influence, and that of the radically reductionist *apriorism* of his follower Euclid, is typical of the problem.

Admittedly, there has been scientific and related progress even among the ranks of reductionists such as some positivists, as in the cases of Karl Weierstrass, his follower Georg Cantor, and David Hilbert, or Hermann Minkowski. This occurs despite the streak of *a-priorism* traced from Euclid, that to the degree that their work represented an attempted reform of, rather than the needed break with the Euclidean hoax of *a-priorism*.[4]

Define true creativity, in both science and in Classical artistic composition, as being the domain of the Classical-artistic modes of the imagination.

This subject pertains to those problems of sense-certainty which arise in ways typified by Johannes Kepler's unique discovery of the general Solar principle of gravitation, as presented in his **The Harmony of the Worlds**. The method presented by Kepler there, uses the asymmetrical motions of respectively visual and harmonic expressions of effects of universal gravitation, to define his uniquely original discovery of the general principle of gravitation for the Solar system.

Kepler's rejection of the foolish, reductionist method of sense-certainty, freed science, by use of the scientific method of contradiction among the experi-

---

3. It is notable that the positivist Hilbert fired both disciples of Bertrand Russell, Norbert Wiener and John von Neumann, from his Göttingen program, for incompetence.

4. The modern conception of non-Euclidean physical curvature is appropriately traced to such examples as Brunelleschi's use of the catenary as a physical principle, as for the crafting of the cupola of Florence's Santa Maria del Fiore, and Nicholas of Cusa's rejection of Archimedes' notion of the quadrature of the circle. See also Carl F. Gauss' warning against the notions of a "non-Euclidean" geometry of the misguided type associated with Lobatchevsky and Jonas Bolyai.

Asian nations such as China have recognized the essential role that economic science-drivers, and notably nuclear power, must play in the future. Shown is the Ling Ao Phase II nuclear power plant's full-scope simulator. The plant is in Shenzhen, Guangdong, about 60 km north of Hong Kong.

ence of the senses, as by Nicholas of Cusa's **De Docta Ignorantia**, and the use of the physical principle of the catenary, by Filippo Brunelleschi for the crafting of the cupola of Florence's Santa Maria del Fiore. It is not the senses which "know," but, rather, the reading of sense-perceptions by means of the creative powers unique to the human mind; it is the man, not his mere footprints, which is the subject of true scientific, and Classical artistic knowledge.

Einstein's appreciation of Kepler's discovery produced the famous notion of a finite, but not bounded universe, otherwise known as an anti-entropic, Riemannian universe.

The lesson to be emphasized in addressing the role of human creativity in the advancement of human life on, and beyond the present bounds of our planet, is typified by the recent century's experience with such transcendental phenomena as nuclear fission and thermonuclear fusion. As the legendary forces of attrition push us away from reliance on what had been considered as competent economic policy, to higher orders of economic science-drivers, we require what should be regarded as that famous principle, that what has passed is attrition, and what must be, is the higher energy-flux densities which are only typified for us today by the notions of nuclear fission and thermonuclear fusion.

On this account, while the trans-Atlantic economies presently regress, chiefly, from fading twilight, toward scientific darkness, the nations of Asia such as China and India, have recognized the essential role of those leaps in progress which must be brought into practice, to overcome the errors inherent in the presumption that each national culture must simply copy the steps made by those cultures gripped by their own adoption of that legacy of decline which has recently come to dominate trans-Atlantic culture. This was the decline which has been oncoming since the decline from the level represented by the leading role of President Franklin Roosevelt during the course of preparing for, and conducting the defeat of the Nazi menace prior to and during what has been referred to as "World War II."

It is the creative powers which distinguish the essential nature of the human beings from that of the beasts, the powers native to the human creative-artistic imagination, the powers on which we must depend for bringing about those seemingly astonishing leaps upward in the human condition throughout the planet, and beyond, on which the escape from the presently menacing collapse into decadence, into which the old Trans-Atlantic order has fallen—we may hope, only temporarily.

Without a shift of outlook, from merely past experience, to the needed discovery of a future, beyond the reach of the past civilization, as a planetary system's phenomenon, we were already doomed to a prolonged, planet-wide dark age of all humanity. It is the challenge of the horrid poverty still met *en masse* in Asia and Africa today, which should become the source of stimulus which will bestir the rescue our planet from a presently, otherwise, inevitable slide into the abyss.

Mueller Issues Fake Indictment; Brits in Fit that Putin, Trump Might Make Peace

The LaRouche Political Action Committee released the following statement by Barbara Boyd on July 13, 2018.

Desperate to head off a possible accommodation between President Trump and President Putin, which could result in a principled approach to a viable peace, the British, Robert Mueller, and the "resist" holdover forces in the U.S. intelligence community and news media have staged a trifecta of calculated information warfare operations within the last 24 hours to sabotage the summit.

Mueller Indicts Russian GRU

In the United States, two interrelated events have occurred: First, embattled FBI Agent Peter Strzok appeared before a joint House hearing on Thursday, July 12, to claim that the Republicans on the House Judiciary and Government Oversight committees were doing "Putin's work" for him by continuing to examine the British and Obama Administration/Democratic Party origins of Russiagate. Strzok's charge, obviously choreographed with Congressional Democrats, was greeted by them with Jacobin cheers, and endlessly cycled in the news media.

The Democrats otherwise sought to obstruct the discredited FBI agent's testimony, by any and all means necessary, to the delight of the fawning news media and the "resist" social media universe. Strzok was the lead FBI case agent on both the Hillary Clinton email investigation and the Trump Russiagate investigation. The Justice Department's independent Inspector General, Michael Horowitz, found that Strzok's prioritization of the Trump Russiagate investigation over the Clinton email investigation was not free from bias, an inconvenient fact largely glossed over in Thursday's staged event. Strzok and his mistress, former FBI Deputy Director Andrew McCabe's counsel, Lisa Page, exchanged daily texts vowing to stop Trump's election, disparaging Trump's supporters, and declaring themselves the saviors of the nation from the catastrophic danger they saw in Trump. Less than 24 hours after the House hearing, Special Counsel Robert Mueller today indicted twelve members of Russia's GRU, the military intelligence branch, for allegedly hacking the DNC, John Podesta, and various other Democratic Party entities, in order to interfere in the 2016 U.S. elections against Hillary Clinton. Russia's alleged cyber activities are, of course, the central premise of Robert Mueller's entire witchhunt against President Donald Trump. Democratic leader Sen. Chuck Schumer immediately demanded that Trump cancel his meeting with Putin based on the indictment. Reached today, after conducting a quick review of Mueller's indictment, former NSA Technical Director William Binney declared the document to be "a fabrication." "The only actual forensic investigations performed on available data regarding 'hacks' of the DNC are independent investigations assessed and approved by a group of us at the Veterans Intelligence Professionals for Sanity," Binney noted. He continued,

The FBI never even bothered to examine the DNC computers, relying instead on the DNC and Atlantic Council cyber contractor CrowdStrike for its evidence. Our analysis demonstrated that the Guccifer 2.0 and DCLeaks personas were created inside the United States. Our analysis also fully demonstrated that the transfer of the information was consistent with a download to a thumb drive, not transmission over the Internet. Separate and apart from the VIPS analysis, Ray McGovern and I have consistently said that available data surrounding charges regarding "Russian hacking" suggest that the CIA's Vault 7 cyber weapons arsenal, enabling false attribution and "tell-tale" signs in Cyrillic and other "obfuscation" may be at work in at least some of this.

Former Director of National Intelligence and former CIA Director John Brennan's benighted views on Russia seem also to be in play over the past several years. Suffice it to add that, despite our assessment of John Brennan's cyber-operations and false attribution programs at the CIA, Brennan's geopolitical fixation on Russiagate, and despite our work with independent forensic analysts (or perhaps because of it), we have never been contacted by Robert Mueller or any Congressional investigative committee.

Since members of the GRU are unlikely to present themselves to the U.S. courts, nothing in Mueller's indictment will ever have to be actually proved in a court of law. The indictment does demonstrate, however, that substantial time was spent in creating a "save the appearances" version of a crime for the credulous, after the Obama intelligence community's initial presentation of an "assessment" of the hack never achieved general credibility beyond very gullible and technically challenged members of the U.S. press corps and the U.S. Congress. Moreover, with all the hullabaloo attached to Mueller's stunt, the fact remains that the DNC and John Podesta emails revealed a stunning and irrefutable truth: Hillary Clinton and the DNC were rigging the election against her Democratic primary opponent, Bernie Sanders. So much for "interference."

'Novichok'—Again

The third element of this coordinated assault on the prospect of peace was the discovery of a bottle or vial of the so-called Novichok nerve agent that had allegedly been used to poison former British spy Sergei Skripal and his daughter Yulia. The bottle was discovered at the home of Charlie Rowley and Dawn Sturgess in Amesbury, England. The British had gone on an international rampage over the March 4, 2018, Skripal poisoning, claiming that it was Putin conducting the murder of a long-retired British spy on British territory in some form of retaliatory action, demanding war-like sanctions against Putin and Russia. When their claims failed to achieve substantive credibility, even with the British bio-weapons lab, Porton Down, Rowley and Sturgess appeared as new victims of the nerve agent poisoning on June 30. Sturgess subsequently died.

The British press is filled with the imputation that the found vial will somehow be traceable back to Russia, a connection which eluded the original Skripal hoax.

Desperate Ploys Won't Work

These are desperate ploys and will not survive scrutiny outside their wave-like propaganda effect on the public mind. Strzok's portrayal of himself as Captain America, hating Putin, hating Trump for being rational about Putin, hating the smell of Trump supporters, deriding the intelligence of every Trump voter, defending the country against the destabilizing destruction represented by Donald Trump, yet somehow able to "follow the facts, wherever they lead," simply did not sell. As even CNN commented, his own text messages, demonstrating both his overt bias and willingness to shape his official actions in that light, were fatally "damning."

www.ingramcontent.com/pod-product-compliance
Lightning Source LLC
Chambersburg PA
CBHW080239260726
48658CB00008B/3166